THE SCIENCE
OF THE PARANORMAL

THE SCIENCE
OF THE
PARANORMAL

The Last Frontier

Lawrence LeShan

THE AQUARIAN PRESS
Wellingborough, Northamptonshire

First published 1984 as *From Newton to ESP*
This Edition, revised, 1987

Ref
BF
1031
.L424
1987

680 68402

British Library Cataloguing in Publication Data

LeShan, Lawrence
The science of the paranormal: the last
frontier. — New ed.
1. Psychical research
I. Title   II. LeShan, Lawrence. From Newton
to ESP
133   BF1031

ISBN 0-85030-628-0

*The Aquarian Press is part of the
Thorsons Publishing Group.*

Printed and bound in Great Britain

CONTENTS

[The new knowledge] . . . frees us from the chains of a
most narrow dungeon and sets us at liberty to rove in a more august empire . . .
of an infinite space, of sc worthy a field, and of such beautiful worlds.
Giordano Bruno

This book is dedicated to my wife Eda, who makes my work possible,
and who makes it worthwhile.

The author wishes to express his deep gratitude
to James S. McDonnell, The McDonnell Foundation,
and The Psychophysical Laboratories for making this book possible.

INTRODUCTION

The world is made up of stories, not of atoms.
Muriel Rukeyser

If Sir Isaac Newton were alive today and sitting under his tree, he would have access to information and concepts undreamed of when he was alive in the seventeenth century. Because of them he would see at least three apples fall where he had previously seen just one.

The first would be the solid, round apple, red and juicy, to which his senses could respond.

The second would be an area filled with 'singularities haunting space', an area filled with very, very small areas having charge, mass and inertia moving at incredible speeds.

The third would be an apple about which it was just as legitimate to say that the Earth was falling towards *it* as to say that *it* was falling towards the *Earth*.

Today, Newton would know that none of these apples was more real than any other.

As the physicist Max Planck put it after he had begun to develop our present-day comprehension of the second apple, we no longer live in a 'single-tracked universe', but in a 'multi-tracked' one. Each of the apples described above is on a different track, in a different realm of experience. There is no contradiction between what we find on each track, but we find very different things. What is impossible and 'paranormal' on one track is perfectly possible and normal on another. Even the meaning of such terms as 'space', 'time' and 'causality' may be different on different tracks.

How many tracks will be useful for science in the future we do not know. Today we are aware of five that are necessary for us to deal effectively with the data that is available. On two of these we observe ESP occurrences. On these tracks such occurrences are perfectly possible and normal. If we understand this and study these occurrences, these 'psi phenomena', as observations made on these tracks, we can make sense of them and learn to use them in our attempts to make a world fit for human beings, and human beings fit for our lovely world.

In the eighteenth century the mystic and poet William Blake recognized the narrowness of Newton's concepts and understood the implications of the theories of Planck and Einstein long before they were formulated. He wrote:

> May God us Keep
> From Single Vision and Newton's Sleep.

Today in science we are just beginning to understand the meaning of Blake's words.

The word 'paranormal', the ideas of ESP, of telepathy, clairvoyance and precognition, tend to make us feel that we are dealing with strange and uncanny things. We picture thoughts floating in space between one person and another, strange mental energies and forces that treat space and time as open roads as they go from person to person, person to thing, and perhaps even from a spirit to a living human being. They seem magical and mythical to us. We may believe in them, but even if we do we also feel that they need a different type of explanation from the everyday things and actions around us. They are bubbles of mystery that seem to float around in an otherwise ordinary universe.

In spite of our efforts to make them scientific by showing that we can detect traces of them, in long series of guesses of concealed cards, by means of elaborate statistical techniques (after all, if it's mathematical, it *must* be scientific), they still seem somehow to belong to an older time – a time long before the Industrial Revolution. Perhaps even to a time of the Older Gods, when the Oracle spoke at the shrine of Apollo at Delphi and kings listened obediently to her words.

It is no wonder, when such feelings are associated with the paranormal, that the scientific community has largely turned its back
on it and refused to give it the hallmark of legitimacy.

It is also no wonder that many people in our time, disenchanted
with the wonders of a scientific establishment that produces so
much pollution of our air and water, that seems to them primarily
bent on producing more and bigger nuclear weapons when we
already have enough to kill every human being on Earth a dozen
times over, have developed an excited and largely uncritical
interest in it, believing everything and wallowing in it as an
antidote to the insane antics of 'science' that they see all around
them.

The problem is that the 'paranormal' is a perfectly normal part of
the human potential, of our relation to others and to the world
around us, but we have so mythologized it, made it so strange and
'other', that we can do nothing with it. We cannot garden this part
of our being – we find ourselves instead uncritically for or against
its existence, and we tend to lose all our common sense when we
approach it.

This is seen, for example, in what usually happens to a 'good
psychic' – a person who has frequent conscious awareness of his or
her own ESP perceptions, and is not afraid of them. When they
reveal this to others and try to explore it, they find themselves torn
in two opposite directions by two kinds of people. On the one hand,
there are those who immediately and enthusiastically believe
everything and constantly plead for new wonders. On the other
hand, there are those who believe nothing and obdurately stick to
the view that the psychic needs a psychiatrist, or a jail sentence for
fraud. Under the stress of these two kinds of pressure ('It is', said
one psychic, 'like living under a shower that constantly and
abruptly changes from very hot to icy cold and back again'), the
psychic typically either becomes completely uncritical towards his
own abilities and keeps trying to produce bigger and better ESP
experiences, or else becomes so hypercritical and angry that he
loses the ability altogether. It takes a psychic of very rare personality, strength and organization to keep a balance in the swirling
emotional currents they produce around them.

Our present attitudes toward the paranormal can be traced to the
Renaissance, when our entire culture made a tremendous and
successful effort to develop a new view – a 'scientific', a

'mathematical' view – of the universe. As part of this we abandoned the magical concept of space that we had used previously –
the space of astrology and hexing, full of 'forces' and 'tendencies' –
and developed a geometric view of space. This space was the
'emptiness' of Newton filled only by bits and pieces of matter. In
the course of this gigantic effort to change our concept of reality,
we threw out a number of babies with the bathwater. Among these
discarded babies was the idea that the paranormal was normal and
could be explained in reasonable terms. Indeed, in the world-view
held by science and the culture generally, from the seventeenth
century through the nineteenth, there was no room for the
paranormal. It could, so this view of the universe held, be believed
in only by primitive and superstitious minds. However, in the
twentieth century, the world-view of science, the scientific belief
as to how-things-work, changed tremendously. One of the
implications of this new view is that *there is nothing surprising or
difficult about ESP,* about telepathy, clairvoyance or precognition.
These are perfectly normal – albeit somewhat unusual –
phenomena. In this view, there is no such thing as a paranormal
phenomenon, although some phenomena are less normal than
others. It is also true that the majority of the scientific community
have not yet perceived this implication.

This is the central point of the present book. This, and the fact
that now new vistas open before us. For the first time, we can
accept this part of the human condition and scientifically study,
understand and develop it as a part of the natural potential of
human beings. We can now learn to use it to further our growth,
our development and our aims. A part of us, previously denied, or
else treated only mythically and magically, can now be brought
closer to fruition. Since this part of us *relates* us to others and to
nature in general, there is a strong possibility that in these areas –
the areas of our greatest problems – the whole picture may change.

I shall start the book with a section on the differences between
normal perception (with the use of the senses) and paranormal
perception (where the senses are not involved). As I shall demonstrate, there are surprisingly *few* differences between them, and no
differences at all that makes one more difficult to accept than the
other from the viewpoint of modern science. In order to be able to
think clearly about the similarities and differences between them, I
shall – in the course of this section – give normal perception the

name 'Type A' perception and paranormal perception the name 'Type B'. Changing our terms in this way, so that we no longer carry along such a load of emotional baggage and preconceptions, will enable us to see more clearly how truly minor the differences are between them.

The book then proceeds to describe the history of psychical research and parapsychology, and why the paranormal was considered scientifically unacceptable from the sixteenth to the nineteenth centuries. I shall then describe the scientific revolution of the twentieth century that has readmitted the paranormal into the halls of the 'real' and show how the new model of science permits us to study and use Type B perceptions. Two examples will be given in detail. One is of a model research programme to be done in the future. The second is of a research programme in teaching psychic healing that has been successfully completed and that has now trained over 400 people in the use of this psychic ability. I conclude with a chapter on what we can legitimately expect in the future from this new development.

This book is the culmination of thirteen years' full-time research into the nature of paranormal phenomena (ESP, clairvoyance, telepathy and precognition), and four years' work with the physicist-philosopher Henry Margenau on the nature and structure of the modern scientific view of how-the-world-works. The work on ESP has led to a dozen or so professional articles and two books, *The Medium, The Mystic and The Physicist* (1974, 1975) and *Alternate Realities* (1976, 1977). The collaboration with Professor Margenau resulted in a jointly authored book, *Einstein's Space and Van Gogh's Sky: Physical Reality and Beyond* (1982 and 1983). The integration of these two projects forms the basis of the present book, which argues that the so-called 'paranormal' is no more strange or 'occult' than the so-called 'normal'. The acquisition of knowledge by ESP no more contradicts the modern scientific view of reality than does the acquisition of knowledge through the use of the senses. The first may be much more rare, but is no more difficult to explain and to understand. Both are equally comprehensible, and equally mysterious.

The study of the paranormal changed radically in the 1930s. Wanting very much to be accepted into the academic and scientific communities, workers in this field tried to become 'scientific'.

They interpreted this to mean fitting their work into the model of nineteenth-century physics rather than twentieth-century science – thereby demonstrating the truth of the statement by the physicist Max Born that 'The physics of one period is the meta-physics of the next'. This led to abandoning research on the kind of phenomena that had aroused our interest in this area, mediumship, death-bed apparitions, telepathic communications of important information, and so forth, which was felt could not be studied in a quantitative manner. Researchers turned instead to the study of guessing concealed cards, mentally influencing the fall of dice, and other experiments in which the results could be quantified. This did not lead to academic or scientific acceptance, nor to scientific progress; but it did succeed in making an exciting and interesting field rather dull and boring.

It is relevant here to mention that my basic field of training is in scientific methodology and experimental design in the social sciences, and that my assumption, when I began work in this area, was that there was *no* valid data relating to the paranormal, since its existence would appear to contradict everything I believed about the nature of reality. As a trained twentieth-century scientist, I was certain that telepathy, clairvoyance and precognition were old wives' tales, and that examination of the reported 'experiments' would show that their designs were faulty.

To my surprise, I found that my prejudices would not hold together when faced with the available data. No matter how critically I attempted to view the experimental evidence, I could not find a way to dismiss it. The only possible alternative to accepting the validity of the data – a vast conspiracy that included some of the most serious scientists of our time – seemed ridiculous. The data were real. When I began to work with the psychic Eileen Garrett and repeatedly observed her producing paranormal phenomena under the most careful scientific conditions (some of these occurrences will be reported later), it was clear to me that ESP was real.

> The famous physicist William Barrett once gave a lecture on Psychical Research. At the end a scientific colleague said, 'A very interesting lecture, Barrett, but it's all tosh, you know.' Barrett replied, 'Well, you are a scientific man. When you have spent as many weeks as I have years studying these subjects, I shall value your opinion.'[1]

Once I had accepted the existence of ESP phenomena, the lack of theory in the field seemed to be the major deficiency, a lack which prevented both scientific acceptance and the development of a research programme for exploring further. Barrett had written in this connection, 'Without a theory, facts are a mob not an army', and the present 'state of the art' appeared to illustrate his point very well.

This book presents an integration of three developments of modern science: the philosophic basis and implications of the Planck-Einstein revolution in physics; the concept of alternate realities of the social sciences; and the work of psychical research and parapsychology. When these three are put together, it becomes obvious that the 'paranormal' is 'normal' and a reasonable part of twentieth-century science and thought. No paradoxes remain. A scientific theory of ESP emerges and our ESP facts begin to become an army, not a mob. The paranormal becomes an acceptable part of the human potential, a part we can now garden and develop.

The field of psychical research, which started out as a great dream and adventure, is now in a sad and depressed state; indeed, it is extremely doubtful whether it can be rescued from this situation by those now working in it. Most of them are apparently hopelessly mired in a bog of outmoded science and philosophy. Hardworking and dedicated, they remind one of no one so much as Cervantes' Don Quixote of La Mancha, who set out on a great quest fully equipped to deal with a world that had long passed away; or perhaps of Gilbert and Sullivan's Modern Major General, who had studied and knew expertly a wide variety of fields, but also said of himself:

> My military knowledge, though I'm plucky and adventurey,
> Has only been brought down to the beginning of the century.

The dream and quest of psychical research was to comprehend those ways in which people are *together*. Other fields studied how they were separate, and even how they interacted as separate entities: psychical research studied the ways in which all human beings were one and could *not* be separated by space, time, perhaps even by death itself. This unbreakable unity, this *oneness*, was the basic focus of the field. Such aspects as crisis telepathy, in which people who sorely needed to communicate but could not do so through speech or signal, *did* communicate, or death-bed apparitions and other major human events of this kind, events that made a difference, were carefully collected and analyzed.

For reasons that will be discussed in some detail later, this aim and methodology were largely abandoned. No more were meaningful human events the focus of study. The analysis of series of meaningless events (such as the study of card guessing, in which the subjects generally did not know when they had made a successful guess and when they had not, and – when they did – could not tell which successes were due to chance and which were due to ESP) took the centre of the stage. The idols of the nineteenth-century laboratory became the guiding principles for research. The advent of computer technology was accepted with great acclaim as presenting a new set of tools that made possible the study of smaller and smaller events in longer and longer series. The Random Number Generator became the tool of choice, as had the Zener cards forty years earlier.

During the time all this had been going on, a quiet and little noticed process has been gaining momentum in western science. This was the movement away from the idea that only one model of the universe was necessary to explain all of reality towards the concept that different models were necessary to deal with different aspects (realms) of experience. It started with Max Planck's demonstration in 1900 that the metaphysical system necessary to explain the microcosm (the world of things too small for the senses to observe, even theoretically) and to make its data meaningful (i.e., to find the laws relating the data) was a different one from the system necessary and valid for the realm of experience of things accessible to the senses. In his words, we live in a 'two-tracked universe'. As the physicist Erwin Schrödinger put it:

> As our mental eye penetrates into smaller and smaller distances and shorter and shorter times, we find nature behaving so entirely differently from what we observe in visible and palpable bodies of our surrounding, that *no* model shaped after our large-scale experiences can ever be 'true'.[2]

A few years later, Einstein showed that a third system, a third model, was necessary for that realm of experience which included things too large, or going by too fast, to be accessible to the senses.

None of these explanatory systems contradict each other. They are compatible. None of them is more or less valid than the others: it is simply accessible to a specific realm of experience. In Goethe's words, 'Nature has neither kernel nor shell.' This means that for the first time data can be examined without preconceptions: we can examine data on their own terms and follow them to whatever laws they lead us. While in the nineteenth century as great a scientist as Lord Kelvin could say that he found it impossible to believe a theory could be valid unless it followed the same laws as a machine, the twentieth-century scientist could develop his theory from the data he observed, without regard to whether they led to a specific model of reality or not.

It gradually became apparent that two other models of how-the-world-works were also necessary to include all of our experience. The first of these was necessary to make the data derived from the meaningful activity of living creatures coherent. We walk down the street to buy a paper, the hare flees, the hound pursues, Mr Babbitt invites a friend to a dinner party, we open and read a book: these are examples of meaningful behaviour and simply cannot be explained on the same principles we must use to deal with the realms of experience of interest to the physicist. For example, a new 'observable' has appeared, one that fits nowhere in these other systems. This is our *purpose* in doing these things. This is as clear an entity in this realm as is *mass* or *electrical charge* in other realms of experience and cannot be validly ignored.

The fifth realm that demands a new system of explanation, a new metaphysical explanatory system, is the realm of consciousness – what goes on in our inner experience. This is a realm in which there are no things, only processes, a realm in which the observables are not quantifiable in principle, and a realm in which there is only 'private access' (only one person can observe the data), as opposed to the 'public access' of other realms, where more than one person can observe the data and in which we can agree, disagree and come to agreements on what it is.

Thus science has now understood that more than one explanatory system is needed to explain our data and experience. In William James's words, we have moved from the belief that we live in a 'universe' to the knowledge we live in a 'pluriverse'.

Parallel to this change in the scientific world-view, another little noticed development was taking place in the social sciences. Here we were beginning to see that human beings organized all of their experience in different ways at different times, and that each of these organizations was valid for some purposes and not for others. When we are dreaming or playing we organize reality far differently from when we are designing an aircraft or finding our location on a street map. When we are praying we use a third organization of reality, and when we are listening to a Beethoven sonata we use a fourth. Here also we are beginning to understand that none of these organizations are inferior to the others; they are each adapted to different purposes. These conclusions have been slowly coming to our attention from anthropology, psychiatry, and psychology, and have been so consistent that they have succeeded in gradually overcoming our resistance to the new idea and our reluctance to give up the older concept that there was only one valid way of organizing reality.

In a larger context, these two developments have meant that science has gradually realized that *we can never know what reality is,* but that we can only perceive and know it after it has been alloyed with, and shaped by, our consciousness. We no longer, in science, search for what reality *is,* but only for the ways that we can most usefully construe it for our purposes. This is probably the most important and – in spite of clear statements by such scientists as Planck, Einstein, Eddington and Margenau – unnoticed development of modern science.

Unfortunately, parapsychologists as a whole do not seem to have been aware of these changes. Theories and experimental designs have typically been on the basis that there was one explanatory system, one correct metaphysical system, and that this was the system that gave nineteenth-century physics and mechanics their tremendous power and authority.

This book will concentrate on the large and meaningful paranormal events that are fascinating because they clearly seem to tell us something new about what it means to be a human being. It will show what these events are, how we can understand and study them and what our legitimate hopes are for the future of work in this area. It will indicate, finally, some of the implications of these events for the question of what it means to be a human being.

1
THE BACKGROUND OF THE PROBLEM

The kind of events that psychical research studies are not new. As far back as human history is recorded we have many examples of telepathy, clairvoyance, precognition, divination, and other psi phenomena. What *is* new is the way we look at these incidents and the methods of investigating them we have designed and used to try to understand them.

In the sixth century before the birth of Christ, the king of the Lydians, Croesus, was thinking about declaring war on a neighbouring kingdom. Needing some expert advice on the outcome, he decided to consult an oracle. The problem was, Which one? There were a number of oracles with excellent reputations for foretelling the future. Since so much was at stake – Croesus's kingdom and possibly his life – he wanted to know which was the most reliable. Croesus therefore devised an experiment to test all the oracles before he relied on one to provide an answer to such a crucial question.

He called together six teams of two men each. Each team was assigned to one oracle. The teams were to leave immediately and on the hundredth day following had to ask their oracles a single question – 'What is Croesus doing at this moment?' In the days before telegraphs and telephones, with the oracles hundreds or thousands of miles away, and with Croesus making up his mind at the very last moment on the hundredth day, this was a well-planned and scientific experiment. Indeed, with the possible exception of asking the oracle to guess a number based on a table of random numbers (which every oracle of the time would have considered to be a trivializing of and an insult to their abilities) it is not easy to see how a modern parapsychology laboratory could have improved on it.

On the hundredth day Croesus made up his mind and did the most unlikely thing he could think of. He put a large bronze pot over a fire and in it put a lamb and a tortoise.

The six teams each wrote down the response of their particular oracle, sealed the tablets they wrote on, and brought them back to the king. Four missed completely. One was partially right. Only one was correct – the oracle at the shrine of Delphi in Greece, which said: 'The king of Lydia has a bronze pot with a bronze lid. In it, over the fire, are a lamb and a tortoise.'*

Here is an excellent example of what we now call ESP. The only thing that has really changed since Croesus's day and ours is our attitude towards such events.

At the time it occurred, the problem of explaining the success of the Delphic oracle was not considered to be a serious one. The information came to the oracle through the gods, and there was an end to the matter (one of the common names for Apollo, to whom the shrine at Delphi was sacred, was Apollo Longsight, or Apollo Farseer). One did not ask *how* the shrines and oracles obtained their information, any more than one asks the Vatican today how, with such a large bird population in the world, God can keep His eye on the individual sparrow. (If one *did* ask such a question, the answer would certainly be that the problem does not lie in the large size of the bird population, but rather in the small size of your conception of God.)

Today, however, the type of explanation that satisfied Croesus has long been unpopular and not to be used in public if you wish to maintain your cultural or scientific status. Therefore, it is now a problem.

What constitutes a problem and what does not depends, in large part, on what period of what culture one is talking about. Before

*The end of the incident is that Croesus then sent another team to Delphi with many rich presents to ask what would happen if he went to war. The oracle answered that 'A great empire would be destroyed'. Croesus went to war, was completely defeated and lost his kingdom. When he later reproached the oracle for giving him false information, the oracle replied that he should have asked *which* empire would be destroyed.

the seventeenth century no one in the West really believed that the relationship between the mind and the body deserved serious study. Darwin considered the problem of the origin of life to be 'rubbish'. The court of Louis XIV frequently debated the question, 'If two perfect painters painted the same model, would their pictures be identical?' We are no more interested in this question today than we are in such questions as 'Do angels know the future?', 'How shall we refute the Albigensian heresy?', or 'If the earth is round, why don't those underneath fall off?' These are questions that deeply concerned some of the keenest minds the human race has ever developed. What is and what is not a problem is a part of the entire cultural pattern; when the pattern changes, so do the questions.

Indeed, the source of ESP information was of little concern until the seventeenth century. (The major exception was the problem of whether such information came from good or bad spirits. This was generally decided on the basis of your relationship to the local power structure. If this relationship was good, then the decision generally was that your information came from God, good spirits, angels or saints; if your relationship was not so good, the decision frequently was that the information came from the devil or one of his assistants, and you would almost certainly end up dying in an unpleasant manner fairly soon.)

In the seventeenth century the prevailing picture of how-things-work began to change rapidly in the West. The new view was that everything in the world worked in the same way – the way in which machines worked. Things only affected each other by direct contact, in the same way that a connecting rod pushes a wheel around. It followed that action-at-a-distance was an unacceptable concept. Once Newton showed how this type of mechanical model could be applied to the movement of the planets, it became increasingly the only acceptable type of explanation until, by the end of the nineteenth century, it had been applied to virtually everything – including the evolution of species, the workings of society and consciousness itself.

With this view, the existence of the soul and its survival of biological death became unacceptable. Machines had no souls and do not survive breakup: the same was therefore true of the human mechanism, which worked in the same way as machines and was subject to the same laws and conditions. Materialism (the philosophy that only what can directly affect your sense organs is real) and mechanism (the theory that everything works on mechanical principles) thus became the prevailing cultural and scientific views. With these views, God, the soul, and the survival of bodily death were neither reasonable nor intelligent ideas.

Not everyone was happy with these developments by any means. A search for scientific evidence to support the non-mechanical view of human beings and the existence of the soul began. In the nineteenth century a number of distinguished minds began a search for evidence that Carlyle was wrong when he spoke of human beings functioning according to the same rules that made a steam engine work. They started to use the methods of science to try and disprove what were generally considered to be the philosophical assumptions and ideas that made science possible. They believed in the existence of the soul and began to try to see if science could corroborate their belief by studying, with the best scientific methodology then available, mediums who claimed that the spirits of dead people communicated through them, thought transference (which would prove, at least, that humans had abilities machines did not), and other phenomena. Psychical research started as a theory in search of facts.[1]

The search revealed two things quite early in its development. The first was that there was a great deal going on that could not be accounted for by the accepted views of contemporary science. There was simply too much evidence of individuals having specific information that they did not get through their senses, or could have deduced from information acquired that way, to ignore. 'Anecdotal' these cases might be – that is, they simply happened to people and were not planned in advance and made to occur in a laboratory – but they were so frequently reported, showed such basic consistencies (that is, they fell into natural classes), and were reported so often by people of very high calibre with no vested interests that to ignore them would have been flying from the evidence.

Typical of these types of cases are the following.

Case 1

The parties concerned were Mr Arthur Severn, a distinguished landscape painter, and his wife; the narrative was obtained through John Ruskin. Mrs Severn wrote:

Brantwood, Coniston
October 27th 1883

I woke up with a start, feeling I had had a hard blow on my mouth, and with a distinct sense that I had been cut and was bleeding under my upper lip, and seized my pocket-handkerchief and held it (in a little pushed lump) to the part, as I sat up in bed, and after a few seconds, when I removed it, I was astonished not to see any blood, and only then realized it was impossible anything could have struck me there, as I lay fast asleep in bed, and so I thought it was only a dream! – but I looked at my watch, and saw it was seven, and finding Arthur (my husband) was not in the room, I concluded (rightly) that he must have gone out on the lake for an early sail, as it was so fine.

I then fell asleep. At breakfast (half-past nine) Arthur came in rather late, and I noticed he rather purposely sat farther away from me than usual, and every now and then put his pocket-handkerchief furtively up to his lip, in the very way I had done. I said, 'Arthur, why are you doing that?' and added a little anxiously, 'I know you have hurt yourself! but I'll tell you why afterwards.' He said, 'Well, when I was sailing, a sudden squall came, throwing the tiller suddenly round, and it struck me a bad blow in the mouth, under the upper lip, and it has been bleeding a good deal and won't stop.' I then said, 'Have you any idea what o'clock it was when it happened?' and he answered, 'It must have been about seven.'

I then told what had happened to me, much to *his* surprise, and all who were with us at breakfast.

It happened here about three years ago at Brantwood to me.

Joan R. Severn

In reply to inquiries Mrs Severn wrote:

There was no doubt about my starting up in bed wide awake, as I stuffed my pocket-handkerchief into my mouth, and held it pressed under my upper lip for sometime before removing it to 'see the blood' – and was much surprised that there was none. Some little time afterwards, the impression was still vividly in my mind, and that as I was dressing I did look under my lip to see if there was any mark.

Mr Severn's account, dated 15 November 1883 is as follows:

Early one summer morning, I got up intending to go and sail on the lake; whether my wife heard me going out of the room, I don't know; she probably did and in a half-dreamy state knew where I was going.

When I got down to the water I found it calm, like a mirror, and remember thinking it quite a shame to disturb the wonderful reflections of the opposite shore. However, I soon got afloat, and as there was no wind contented myself with pulling up my sails to dry, and putting my boat in order. Soon some slight air came, and I was able to sail about a mile below Brantwood, then the wind dropped, and I was left becalmed for half an hour or so, when, on looking up to the head of the lake, I saw a dark blue line on the water. At first I couldn't make it out, but soon saw that it must be small waves caused by a strong wind coming. I got my boat as ready as I could, in the short time, to receive this gust, but somehow or other she was taken aback, and seemed to spin round when the wind struck her, and in getting out of the way of the boom, I got my head in the way of the tiller, which also swung round and gave me a nasty blow in the mouth, cutting my lip rather badly, and having become loose in the rudder it came out and went overboard. With my mouth bleeding, the mainsheet more or less round my neck, and the tiller gone, and the boat in confusion, I could not help smiling to think how suddenly I had been humbled almost to a wreck, just when I thought I was going to be so clever! However, I soon managed to get my tiller, and, with plenty of wind, tacked back to Brantwood, and making my boat snug in the harbour, walked up to the house, anxious of course to hide as much as possible what had happened to my mouth, and, getting another handkerchief, walked into the breakfast room, and managed to say something about having been out early. In an instant my wife said, 'You don't mean to say you have hurt your mouth?' or words to that effect. I then explained what had happened and was surprised to see some extra interest on her face, and still more surprised when she told me she had started out of her sleep thinking she had received a blow in the mouth! and that it was a few minutes past seven o'clock, and wondered if my accident had happened at the same time; but as I had no watch with me, I couldn't tell, though on comparing notes, it certainly looked as if it had been about the same time.

Arthur Severn[2]

Case 2

The percipient's half-brother (she refers to him as her brother), an airman, had been shot down in France on the 19th March, 1917, early in the morning. She herself was in India. 'My brother,' she says, 'appeared to me on the 19th March, 1917. At the time I was either sewing or talking to my baby – I cannot remember quite what I was doing at that moment. The baby was on the bed. I had a very strong feeling that I must turn round; on doing so I saw my brother, Eldred W. Bowyer-Bower. Thinking he was alive and had been sent out to India, I was simply delighted to see him, and turned round quickly to put my baby in a safe place on the bed, so that I could go on talking to my brother; then turned again and put my hand out to him, when I found he was not there. I thought he was only joking, so I called him and looked everywhere I could think of looking. It was only when I could not find him I became very frightened and the awful fear that he might be dead. I felt very sick and giddy. I think it was 2 o'clock the baby was christened and in the church I felt he was there, but I could not see him. Two weeks later I saw in the paper he was missing. Yet I could not bring myself to believe he had passed away.[3]

Case 3

Another case . . . is that of the will of James L. Chaffin, a North Carolina farmer who in November 1905 made a will attested by two witnesses in which he left his farm to his son Marshall, the third of his four sons, and nothing to the other three sons or to his wife. In January 1919, however, he made a new will, not witnessed but legally valid because it was wholly in his own handwriting. In it he first stated that it was being made after his reading of the 27th chapter of Genesis, and then that he wanted his property divided equally between his four children, and that they must take care of their mother. He then placed this will at the 27th chapter of Genesis in a Bible that had belonged to his father, folding over the pages to enclose the will.

He died in 1921, without ever having mentioned to anybody the existence of the second will. The first will was not contested and was probated by its beneficiary. But some four years later the second son, James Pinkney Chaffin began to have some very vivid dreams that his father appeared to him at his bedside, without speaking. Later in June of 1925, however, the father again appeared at the bedside, wearing a familiar black overcoat, and then spoke, saying, 'You will find my will in my overcoat pocket.' The coat was eventually found in his brother's house and examined. The inside lining of the inside pocket had been stitched together. On cutting the stitches, James found a little roll of paper on which, in his father's handwriting, were written only the words: 'Read the 27th chapter of Genesis in my daddie's old Bible.' James then returned to his mother's house, accompanied by his daughter, by a neighbour, and by the neighbour's daughter. When they found the Bible and opened it at the 27th chapter of Genesis, they found the second will. It was admitted to probate in December of the same year.

Whether apparitions of the dead really are evidence for survival, however, is made dubious by the fact that there are a good many cases on record of apparitions of persons who were living and in good health at the time. Another fact, which also has to be taken into account in connection with apparitions is that they always wear clothes of some sort; and hence that, as someone has put it, if ghosts have clothes, then clothes have ghosts! This suggests that apparitions, especially when perceived by several persons, may be mental images which, strangely, have become somehow concrete enough to be visible.[4]

Case 4

Not only were individual cases studied, collections of cases concerning specific events were also made. One such collection was made by J. C. Barker, a psychiatrist who visited Aberfan on the day after the terrible disaster that killed 144 people, among them 128 school children (Barker, 1967). At approximately 9.15 a.m. on 21 October 1966, a huge coal tip, rendered unstable by underground water, slid down a mountainside on to the little mining village of Aberfan in Wales. Most of the school children who died were at Pantglas Junior School, which was partially overwhelmed by the sludge, in some places to a depth of forty feet. The children at their desks, or playing, were buried under the black slag. Other victims were claimed by the unstoppable avalanche when it poured across homes in Moy Street, smashing them and burying their unfortunate inhabitants alive.

As Barker worked, he was appalled by the devastation and suffering, and it occurred to him that there might have been people who had premonitions of the disaster. Having been a keen student of psychical phenomena for many years, it struck him that the unusual features of the Aberfan tragedy might provide an opportunity to investigate precognition. A public appeal, through newspapers and other media, brought seventy-six letters to Barker, and he began the long, tedious, but necessary, process of replying, not only to the writers but also to those witnesses who could confirm, if possible, that the writers' experience had been told to them before the Aberfan disaster occurred. In due course, he received confirmation in twenty-four cases. A full report was deposited by Barker in the Archives of the Society for Psychical Research. Space forbids reproducing many of these cases, but one of them can be given.

Eryl Jones, age 10, was a pupil at Pantglas school and died in it. She was the youngest daughter of Trevor and Megan Jones. A local minister, the Rev. Glannant Jones, compiled a report of the case. Both parents signed it as correct in his presence:

She was an attractive, dependable child, not given to imagination. A fortnight before the disaster, she said to her mother, 'Mummy, I am not afraid to die.' Her mother replied: 'Why do you talk of dying, and you so young; do you want a lollipop?' 'No,' she said, 'but I shall be with Peter and June [schoolmates].' The day before the disaster, she said to her mother, 'Mummy, let me tell you about my dream last night.' Her mother answered gently, 'Darling, I've no time now. Tell me again later.' The child replied, 'No Mummy, you *must* listen. I dreamt I went to school and there was no school there. Something black had come down over it!'

The next day off to school went her daughter as happy as ever. In the communal grave she was buried with Peter on one side and June on the other.

This last point may not, however, be significant, since the order of burial was apparently influenced by parents' requests.[5]

Case 5

The year was 1917 and my father-in-law was in the army. On a furlough from Fort Dix, he and a friend had come into New York to see a Wednesday matinée of the James Barrie play, *Dear Brutus*. The title of the play is a quotation from Shakespeare – 'The fault, dear Brutus, is not in our stars but in ourselves that we are underlings.' The play was about a group of people who were given a chance to live their lives over again in a different way. The play was deeply moving (there was a lovely young girl of seventeen in the cast by the name of Helen Hayes!) and my father found himself thinking of his younger brother Jack. His heart ached for Jack who had made the decision to be a farmer, who loved the occupation, but was terribly lonely running a farm alone in an isolated area where there were no other young people. As my father watched the play, he kept thinking to himself, 'How I wish Jack could have a second chance and change his life.'

The next day my father-in-law received a letter from Jack, begging him to come and visit him on his farm because he needed help in deciding what to do with his life. My father-in-law went immediately and as they were having lunch together, Jack suddenly said, 'The fault, dear Brutus, is not in our stars but in ourselves that we are underlings.' My father-in-law was startled and asked his brother what had made him say that. Jack replied, 'It's the strangest thing; I can't even remember where that quote is from, but on Wednesday, while I was milking the cows at about four in the afternoon, I suddenly saw those words on the wall of the barn, as clear as day.' That was the exact moment when my father-in-law, sitting in the theatre, had been thinking about his brother.[6]

The first thing that became evident in the search to prove the existence of the soul was how much needed investigating: the second was that there was a fundamental problem in trying to prove the existence of the soul and of spirits who communicate 'evidential' information. This was the 'super-ESP' problem.

It went like this. A medium claims to have let her consciousness be taken over by a spirit of someone's dear departed and then, talking in a voice very reminiscent of that person (whom she has never met – at least in the flesh), she says things that no one but the dear departed of the sitter and the sitter himself could know. Does this 'evidential' material prove that the spirit is really there and communicating, or is it possible that the medium has picked up the material and the voice patterns telepathically (we do know that, whether or not the soul exists, telepathy *does* happen) and is consciously or unconsciously dramatizing them? Thus anything a medium says falls into one of two possible classes: it can either be verified (i.e., it is known to some person, or is recorded somewhere), or it cannot. If it cannot be verified it is evidentially worthless; if it *can* be verified, the medium may be picking up the information by telepathic or clairvoyant perception. You cannot prove the existence of surviving spirits from mediums unless you know the limits of ESP. Take, for example, the following case.

There was a man living in the western part of the United States who had been a physician and a philanthropist. After his death, his widow and his sister decided to write a biography of him. All went well, except for the first section, which was a disaster, and the more they worked on it, the worse it got. Because of this the manuscript was rejected by publishers who were otherwise interested in it.

At that time I was working closely with Eileen Garrett, one of the greatest psychics of this century. She had never met Dr X, his wife or his sister, but many years ago had had a brief correspondence with the sister, who had read some of Eileen's books and admired her. Knowing that Eileen had a small publishing house, Helix Press, she decided to call on her in New York.

I met the widow and the sister with Eileen at the Parapsychology Foundation and we discussed the problem of getting the biography of Dr X published. Then I had an idea. I suggested that the first section of the book should be tape recorded and then played back to Eileen, who would go into trance and try to get the spirit of Dr X to 'come through', that is, speak through her voice. We would then let 'him' correct the first section. The arrangements were duly made.

The next morning we went into the 'seance room', in which we had two tape recorders and a shorthand secretary, and Eileen went into trance – that is, she manipulated her breathing and her consciousness, her head fell back on to the back of the couch, and she appeared to be unconscious. In a few moments (probably about thirty seconds) she raised her head and, speaking in a different tone and speech pattern, identified herself as 'Uvani' (her 'gatekeeper', who always appeared first in any trance and decided what was possible and what was not for a particular session. He claimed to be an Arab who had been killed by a Turk in 1851 and was an amazingly consistent persona in trance transcripts over a fifty-year period).

Uvani, speaking in his usual 'stage Persian' ('Greetings, Sahib...', and so on), asked what was wanted and I asked if we could talk to Dr X. He replied, as he usually did if we asked to speak to a specific spirit, 'One moment, I'll see if he is around'! (Where, I always wondered, was 'around'? And if he was not 'around', where was he?)

Eileen then appeared to become unconscious again and when, twenty or thirty seconds later, she seemed to recover consciousness she was speaking in a different voice and with a different speech pattern, which both the sister and the widow immediately identified as belonging to Dr X.

Dr X called the widow by pet names she claimed only the two of them knew and recalled incidents that had the sister screaming that they were known only to the two of them. At the end of half an hour each of them was holding one of Eileen's hands and talking animatedly, and very convincingly, to Dr X.

I said at this point that it was time to go to work. I put on both tape recorders, one with a blank tape and recording, the other playing the first section of the book. Every few minutes Dr X would interrupt with suggested changes. As soon as he started to talk I would turn off the playback machine but continued to record. In this way we had a complete running record of the session duplicated by the shorthand secretary. (The editorial changes made by Dr X seemed to me, then and afterwards, to be excellent ones. It should be said here, however, that Eileen had been a professional editor for several years during her life.)

From my own experience with Eileen's trance work, I had learned that during this period of her life, if she stayed in trance for up to one and a half hours she would wake up as refreshed as if she had taken a long nap. If she stayed in trance any longer she would awaken exhausted and drained. At the end of an hour and a quarter, therefore, I said, 'We will have to stop now. We can continue tomorrow.'

Dr X replied: 'Hell, no, we're not going to stop. I've waited five years for this.'

I said: 'Dr X, I am concerned about the health of the instrument.'

He replied: 'Young man, I'm a physician and you're not. I know more about health than you do. Furthermore, I'm in here and you're not, and I know a lot more about what's going on than you do.'

In a moment I was in the midst of an argument with a man who claimed to have been dead for five years. It was a confusing situation to say the least.

After the argument had gone on for a while, I said: 'Dr X, I have no way to get you out. But if you aren't gone in thirty seconds, I'm going to turn off the tape recorder and erase the tape and all the work we have done will be for nothing.'

He replied, 'Okay, if you will agree that we finish this section and start promptly tomorrow at 10 o'clock.'

I agreed. We finished the section in five minutes. Dr X said, 'See you tomorrow at ten.'

After the widow and sister had left I talked to Eileen about the session and I told her (she had, as usual, no conscious memory of the trance period) how certain the two women had been that they were talking to Dr X, and how she had described incident after incident that she could not have known by normal means, and how much her voice and voice patterns had changed. She said something I have always remembered. 'Never forget, Larry, that awake or in trance, I am very telepathic, and that the stage lost a great actress in me!' Here was one of the greatest psychics ever known to science, a deeply serious woman who spent the last thirty years of her life trying to understand what her mediumship was all about, a woman who, during those thirty years, worked almost entirely under experimental conditions with any scientist who would work with her, saying that she did not know whether her paranormal information was derived from spirits of the dead or telepathy.

We have been unable to solve the problem of the source of 'spirit information'. The dilemma may be, perhaps, summed up in another incident involving Eileen Garrett. Shortly before her death, I said to her:

'Eileen, for most of your life, you have been trying to understand what your mediumship was all about. During that time you have consistently gone into trance and spoken as if spirits were communicating through you. What do you, after all this work, really think about these spirits?'

She thought for several minutes and then said:

'Larry, I have to answer you in what seems to be a light and humorous way, but it's the best I can do. It's as if on Monday, Wednesday and Friday I think that they are actually what they claim to be. And as if on Tuesday, Thursday and Saturday, I think they are multiple personality split-offs I have invented to make my work easier. And as if on Sunday, I try not to think about the problem.'

It was not only Eileen who failed to solve the problem; the same is true of the entire field of psychical research. The feeling one gets when a good medium is in trance and talking as though she were the spirit of someone biologically dead is frequently very convincing. It can feel so real that it curls your hair. However, since the scientific view today is that a belief in spirits is, at best, rank superstitition, and since parapsychologists want very much to be thought of as scientists, the problem has been abandoned. The general assumption is that the results of trance mediumship are attributable to telepathy and clairvoyance. By saying this we assume we have solved the problem.

Perhaps this is not altogether a bad way to proceed at this point: for example, if we take the other hypothesis, we are faced with the same problem when we ask how spirits can be telepathic and clairvoyant, and so cannot avoid dealing with it. But in opting for what appears to be the 'scientific' hypothesis we should understand that we are no nearer to a complete solution than Eileen Garrett was: we have simply accepted the solution most in line with the popular metaphysics of our time.

In any case, it has proved impossible to solve the problem of human survival of bodily death through the utterances and behaviour of mediums. Instead, we were left with the new problems of telepathy, clairvoyance and precognition. We brought these into the laboratory and found that we could produce there evidence that these phenomena existed. In the laboratory they existed in minute quantities only, in such situations as a subject guessing more concealed cards correctly than could be attributed to chance. With modern statistical techniques, and with the precision methods of science, we began to work with these. We had no idea how these things could happen, but we could prove they did. Various theoretical models were suggested, but none proved fruitful. We accumulated a tremendous number of experiments demonstrating their existence. We found that more correct guesses came consistently in certain parts of long series of guesses than they did in others. We found that certain researchers were more likely to get good results and others were the opposite. We found that the atmosphere of the laboratory had an effect. We found that the subject's belief systems about the possibility of the existence of psi (psychic abilities) had an effect. We found a great many facts, but could not tie them together. Parapsychology, indeed, became a collection of facts in search of a theory.

When psychical research moved into the laboratory and became parapsychology it left most of its phenomena outside the door. This made for a difficult research position. It is as if geology decided that, since it could not do repeatable experiments outside (it is *so* hard to repeat an earthquake on demand), it would work only in the laboratory on the analysis of what material it could bring inside. No longer would it consider the analysis of geological strata or other configurations in the field. We would expect little progress from such a frightened and self-restricted science.

It *must* be clearly understood that progress and new discoveries are not necessarily functions of precise laboratory technique and scientific method. Indeed, in many situations, these may *impede* progress. New ideas are messy and boorish in relation to well-established theories and techniques. They do not fit in and are likely to be discarded as irrelevant and meaningless. If a new idea or fact comes into our spotless and well-organized scientific work-room, we are likely to respond by shutting the doors and windows even more tightly, rather than by examining our difficult visitor. The highly sterilized laboratory and its methodologies are necessary to refine old ideas and make them more precise, but they are resistant to welcoming new ones.

Alexander Fleming discovered penicillin in 1927 in a small, untidy, ill-equipped laboratory in St Mary's Hospital in London. The mould was a contaminating agent in his experiments.

> On a post-war visit to a spotless aseptic American laboratory processing his drug, Fleming was asked what he thought of the technological advances. The humble Scot replied: 'I'm afraid my mould would have been too frightened to come through one of your windows.'[7]

Gordon Murphy, one of our leading parapsychologists, wrote:

> It seems to me that perspective [in parapsychology] has been lost as fast as specialized skills have been developed. I do not see that issues are grasped or methods developed impressively better in 1966 than in 1928.[8]

Psychical research developed in the late nineteenth century at a time of rising materialism. In the face of a growing belief that only what you could see and touch was real, that all things, living and non-living, worked on a mechanical principle, that death meant annihilation, a search began for evidence that more than the visible existed; that there was more to man than the body; that there was something that survived death.

In the view of one of its founders, Frederic Myers, it was a 'subject which lies at the meeting place of religion, philosophy, and science, whose business it is to grasp all that can be grasped of the nature of human personality'. It was a search for evidence that man was more than a machine, more than could be accounted for by a materialistic philosophy.

Ultimately (in the 1930s), it became clear that there were two types of paranormal activity. The first were the events that had originally excited our interest in the field – the death-bed apparitions, the mediumship cases, the telepathic exchanges that changed our lives. These types of events were non-quantifiable and, it quickly became clear, could never be quantified, partly because they *were* meaningful and *did* affect us. (How would you measure in units the important events of your life – your first love, the death of a parent, the birth of your first child?) The second type of paranormal events were the ones that could be quantified: How many cards could you guess correctly above chance from a concealed deck? How many more times than chance could you make the '5' face of a dice come up by force of will alone? These were small and essentially meaningless events; they had no effect on our lives and, indeed, we rarely knew when they had occurred: we could not tell when we had guessed a concealed card correctly and when we had not. Only with statistical techniques could we reveal that paranormal activity had occurred. These individual guesses were uninteresting and meaningless in themselves; only when studied in a large group could we see anything of interest.

But they *were* quantifiable. The science and thought of our century told us that if we wanted to be 'scientific', if we wanted to study 'real' things, we had to study quantifiable things. We turned away from the big, meaningful, paranormal events that had first interested us in this field, and concentrated on the small and quantifiable ones. We forgot all about why we had embarked on this field of research and focused only on the details of what had happened in the laboratory. We had absolutely no idea *how* people could sometimes correctly guess concealed cards; we knew only that they did. We had an immense amount of data and no way to account for it. Psychical research, which had started as a theory in search of facts, turned into parapsychology, a collection of facts in search of a theory.

One reason for the lack of public interest in the doings of the Societies for Psychical Research in Britain and America at a time of great public interest in the paranormal becomes clear. It is because the Societies, in their quest for 'scientific' status, have taken the heart out of the field. In this connection, in his *Will to Believe*, William James wrote of 'those who are indifferent to Science because Science is so callously indifferent to their concerns'.

And let no one doubt that the present lack of interest is real. At a time of dozens of periodicals and organizations focusing on paranormal matters, the libraries of the official organizations are so deserted that you could hunt moose in them on an average weekday afternoon. Both the British Society for Psychical Research and the American Society are practically moribund due to a lack of public interest.

The truth is that the philosophic ideas of mechanism and determinism – the heart and basis of modern psychology – have as little to do with human experience as do the Random Number Generators and card-guessing experiments of the modern parapsychology laboratory. Both are divorced from human experience and have become remarried to nineteenth-century physical science. These second marriages are essentially sterile and have brought forth no viable children.

Let us try an analogy that is somewhat closer to home. Suppose that a large project were set up to study the phenomena of 'falling in love'. There was an abundance of 'anecdotal cases' that excited our interest in this; the phenomenon was widely reported by individuals and in literature. It was decided that this project must be done according to nineteenth-century concepts of science. Males and females were brought into the laboratory, and delicate scales measured their attraction and repulsion to each other. They were presented to each other under varying conditions, including with and without the ingestion of coffee, alcohol and barbiturates. Eventually, a few 'good subjects' were found (these were strongly attracted to many members of the opposite sex, and in turn attracted many others).

Since no way was found to quantify the anecdotal accounts (although several extensive population surveys showed the phenomenon to be widely reported and often lead to marked changes in behaviour and living and sleeping quarters), it was decided to ignore these as being unscientific and to focus all energy on the laboratory reports. These showed enough signs of mutual attraction on the delicate measuring scales (and a rare case or two of the full phenomenon apparently happening under laboratory conditions) that it could be concluded that the phenomenon did exist, although it was very erratic and rare. Experimenters would spend more and more time varying the conditions in the laboratory and devising more and more sensitive measuring instruments. They would continually try to devise a 'repeatable experiment' (which, they would insist, is the hallmark of 'real science'). In this hypothetical experiment, subjects would, in the laboratory, always demonstrate the existence of the phenomenon by *always* falling in love with each other. The scientists would feel very inadequate that they had not produced such an experiment and would keep on trying.

Some years before this, academic psychology had done much the same thing as parapsychology. Finding that its main area of interest, the centre of its field – consciousness – was non-quantifiable, it stopped studying it and started instead to study things that could be measured; how many combinations of a bell and a puff of air at the eye caused one to blink at the sound of the bell; how many nonsense syllables could be learned in a week with two study periods of a half hour each day compared to the number learned with one one-hour daily period; how many errors a rat made at each choice point in a maze when it was hungry, and how many it made when it was not but was motivated only by the desire to get back to its cage. The study of consciousness and of large, meaningful events in the life of an individual was abandoned. It was rarely mentioned that a science fleeing from its major data because it did not live up to preconceived notions as to what that data *should be* was fundamentally unscientific.[9]

As Sigmund Koch, perhaps our most eminent student of the philosophy of modern psychology, summed up his thirty-year study of the field:

> The entire 100-year course of 'scientific psychology' can now be seen as a succession of changing doctrines about *what* to emulate in the natural sciences ... [This was done] as a security fetish, bringing assurance to the psychologist, and hopefully to the world, that he was a scientist.[10]

This path looked attractive to the psychologist, and even more so to the parapsychologist. The physical sciences had immense prestige and produced dramatic results. As a path, however, it was self-defeating. The best way to *avoid* being, or being recognized as, a scientist is to follow the methods of another discipline and not those relevant to your data. You are not a scientist if you use optical apparatus to study sound: 'Consciously and purposely, psychology in the first half of this century set out to model itself after the paradigms of physics. The result was the "robot-model" of man. . . .'[11] As late as 1953, B. F. Skinner could write: 'The hypothesis that man is *not free* is essential to the application of scientific method to the study of human behaviour [italics his].'[12]

This is the heart of the matter: the idea that scientific method is ultimately the method of the nineteenth-century physicist; the concept that there is only one meaning to the term 'rational', and that since we know what this means in the sensory realm, we also know what it means in all other realms. We know enough about clocks and bicycles to know that they are not free. Therefore when we know enough about human beings we will inexorably find that they are not free either. However, it is just this concept – that the same observables will be found in different realms of experience if we know enough – that science has had to abandon since the Planck-Einstein revolution. We know, for example, that the following statement, which sounds just as reasonable as Skinner's statement above, is false.

> The hypothesis that the movement of an entity in space can be differentiated from its movement in time is essential to the application of the scientific method to the study of stellar masses.

If we accepted it as true, we would have to throw out the theory of relativity. Similarly, the statement:

> The hypothesis that it is possible to accurately determine both the movement and the position of an entity is essential to the application of the scientific method to the study of sub-atomic particles,

if accepted as true, would necessitate our discarding quantum mechanics.

The essential problem of the 'paranormal' was that its occurrence violated one of the Basic Limiting Principles of our society's cherished beliefs about the universe – that there can be no such thing as action-at-a-distance. A woman in Boston sees an apparition of her son, soaking wet and with a bruise on his forehead, and tells others about it. Some days later she receives a letter from the Navy telling her that her sailor son fell overboard in Hawaii at the time she had the vision, struck his forehead on the anchor chain and drowned. A man in Durham, North Carolina, guesses cards at the same time that they are looked at by a man in Yugoslavia: the American correctly guesses too many cards for his performance to be attributable to chance and then reveals he was somehow related to what was happening in Dubrovnik. As we worked more and more with the card-guessing, quantifiable types of events, we seemed to get more deeply involved in speculating about para*physics* rather than para*psychology*. We became increasingly concerned with the problem of how the information got across the distance and how we could avoid the action-at-a-distance paradox.[13] Science as a whole took the stance that, in spite of the field data, there were no paranormal events. When faced with a contradiction between a theory (what is possible and what is impossible) and a set of facts (the data of Psychical Research and Parapsychology), science preferred to hold on to the theory and ignore the facts. This type of procedure may be good for the comfort and ease of mind of scientists. It is certainly not good for the search for truth.

Faced with the same paradox, the parapsychologists *knew* their data was real, and so had to adopt a different strategy. They followed the method of Newton. First, select what is quantifiable. Relate this to other quantifiable things. Make tables of correlations of these relationships, make no attempt to hypothesize (when asked how gravity could operate at a distance, Newton replied, 'Hypotheses non fingo – I don't make hypotheses') and hope that something will turn up to 'explain' the data. In practice, this meant relating the number of cards guessed correctly to such things as specific scores on personality and intelligence tests administered to sender and receiver, to the distance between the sender and receiver, or to the amounts of caffeine or alcohol each had imbibed.

Psychology and parapsychology followed much the same course, turning away from the big, non-quantifiable data (consciousness, crisis telepathy, etc.) towards the smaller, quantifiable material (reflexes, card-guessing, etc.). But today a new and reverse development is taking place in academic psychology.

A growing trend in Western psychology in the past decade has been a recognition of the limitations of laboratory experimentation. The major journal in this field, *The American Psychologist,* has had a number of leading articles on the subject. As long ago as 1960, Orne pointed out that subjects in a laboratory behave in quite different ways from outside the laboratory.[14] Their behaviour is organized in very different ways. For example, there is less seeking for meaning, less self-actualizing behaviour, more obedience to authority, less use of 'distal' and more of 'proximal' cues, less response to the social structure and mores of their society, and so forth. Egon Brunswik has introduced the term 'ecological validity' to denote a concept with which one should evaluate an experiment.[15] A book by Harré and Secord carefully analyzed the differences between what happens in the laboratory and what happens in 'real life', and though they were writing about social psychology, their comments apply equally to parapsychology. They point out, and demonstrate in detail, that it is only by including and analyzing the social context of interpersonal events that any real understanding of these events can be gained. Who could make sense out of the hysterical paralysis of a soldier's rifle arm in a battle situation, in which major factors such as fear of death, guilt, the death of a comrade, and the high *esprit-de-corps* of his unit were operating, by any laboratory stimuli pattern? Ignoring 'real life' and social contexts, laboratory experiments 'really tell us nothing about the events themselves'.[16] (See also references 17 and 18 for more material on this approach.)

SUMMARY

This is the situation that psychical research has been in during the last fifty years at least. We have a large number of facts and this number increases every time the new journals come out. We have no useful or fruitful ways of organizing these facts.

As I shall try to demonstrate in this book, the problem has seemed insoluble because of an assumption deeply built into the thinking of modern society, an assumption that has been abandoned in physics since 1900. This is the concept that there is only one correct meaning to the word 'rational', and that the explanations for psi phenomena have to be the same as the ones we use to describe how a bicycle works. In the following chapters I shall be exploring the history of this idea and its application to the understanding of the paranormal.

We shall begin by clarifying the term 'paranormal'. How does a 'paranormal occurrence' differ from a 'normal occurrence'? In other words, what are the differences between situations in which information is received via the senses, and those in which it is not?

So as not to prejudice our investigation in advance, let us rename these two types of perception in neutral terms. Instead of the term 'normal perception', let us use the term 'Type A perception'. We shall call 'paranormal perception' 'Type B perception'. Without the emotional luggage of the concepts of 'normal' and 'para-normal', we may be able to see more clearly.

2
THE 'NORMAL' AND THE 'PARANORMAL'

It is curious to reflect that the things which man understands best are, on the whole, the things which least concern him. He can predict the movements of the planets, but not the weather, he has fathomed the deep sea, but cannot measure his own desires, he knows more about beer than about his blood ... and the heart of all his knowledge is a mystery, namely, how he gets it.[1]

C. K. Ogden

With these examples of the kind of psi occurrence that first focused our attention on Type B perceptions, we come to the question of how they differ from 'normal' Type A perceptions. What distinguishes these two kinds of events from each other?

Certainly they *are* different. We feel this strongly. But wherein does the difference lie?

Let us start this exploration by asking a simple question. What is the difference between conditions favouring the occurrence of identifiable Type A and of identifiable Type B perceptions? We have been studying normal, Type A, perceptions in the psychology laboratory for a hundred years now. What conclusions have been reached in these studies that are different from the conclusions reached in the study of paranormal, Type B, perceptions?

To our surprise, we find there are no differences. Conditions favouring the occurrence of Type A perceptions also favour the occurrence of Type B. We might begin with the conclusions of Gardner Murphy, who spent a lifetime of study in both fields, and who was president both of the American Psychological Association and of the American Society for Psychical Research.

> We make contact through the sensory processes and through the extrasensory processes in essentially the same way . . . as far as psychology is concerned, the basic dynamics are the same in the two areas. Anything which helps us, for example, to perceive clearly at the level of normal perception helps us to perceive clearly at the level of extrasensory perception.

Murphy goes on to say:

> The same general laws which hold in all psychology, laws relating to the structuring of the world of perception, relating to the influence of motivation upon such structuring, relating to the Gestalt principles of membership, character, closure, salience, relating to the satiation of motives and the role of substitutes during such satiation . . . may be found to apply perfectly to paranormal perception.[2]

Elsewhere he wrote:

> My own point of view would be simply that [in psychology and in parapsychology] we are dealing with the same classes of phenomena all the way through; that the motive power is the same in both fields; that whatever we learn from one type of investigation offers hypotheses which have a very large likelihood of being fulfilled when tried out in the other sphere.[3]

Similarly, summing up his long and rich studies, René Warcollier wrote: 'In our investigations we have observed that the laws of normal and abnormal psychology apply to telepathy.'[4]

John Beloff, one of our most experienced and searching parapsychologists makes the same point: 'What happens . . . in ESP or PK . . . is essentially of the same nature as that which happens in our normal cognitive processes or in our normal voluntary behaviour.'[5]

And J. B. Rhine, the central and most important research specialist in modern parapsychology, wrote:

> [Psi] . . . has already been found to show some of the familiar characteristics of such cognitive abilities as memory and learning. It responds positively to motivation and conditions favouring concentration of effort. Favourable attitudes toward psi capacity, toward the experimenter and toward the test situation appear rather uniformly to improve the operation of psi. The position of a

given trial in the test structure reflects much the same configura-
tional principles and pattern effects found in familiar cognitive
behaviour. For example, tests involving a column of targets are
likely to show greater success at the beginning and end of the
column...on the whole, the relationship of ESP scores to attitudes,
school grades, intelligence quotients, extroversion, and the like
show sufficient consistency to give assurance that a natural
function of the personality is involved.[6]

Among others who have come to this conclusion – that 'normal'
and 'paranormal' perceptions are the same in structure – are
Ducasse,[7] Thouless and Weisner,[8] and Moncrief.[9]

It would be easy to multiply such quotations and to review the
long years of careful laboratory experimentation that led to them.
It does not seem necessary, however, to do this here. The facts are
clear. Psychological and social conditions favouring 'normal'
perception also favour 'paranormal' perception. Psychological and
social conditions operating against normal perception also operate
against paranormal perception. What then are the differences
between them? To our surprise, we shall be able to find only two:
(1) the location of the mystery; (2) the frequency of observed
phenomena. Let us take these one at a time.

In each type of information there is a tremendous gap in our
knowledge of how we acquired the information. In Type A
(normal perception) the gap concerns how the changes in our brain
brought about by sensory stimulation were changed into conscious
experience. We have brain changes. We then have conscious
experience. These two resemble each other about as much – in
A. S. Eddington's phrase – as a telephone number resembles a
subscriber. How is one translated into the other? We do not know.
The gap remains, for the time being, unbridgeable.

> Some influence . . . plays on the extremity of a nerve, starting a
> series of physical and chemical changes which are propagated
> along the nerve of a brain-cell; there a mystery happens, and an
> image or sensation arises in the mind which cannot purport to
> resemble the stimulus which excited it.[10]

In Type B (paranormal perception) the gap is just as large. How
does the information get from the original source to consciousness?
I suddenly know that my daughter, 500 miles away, has had a car
accident. I even know correctly some of the details. How did the

knowledge cross the 'gap'? We do not know. The gap remains, for the time being, unbridgeable.

It is, to use an analogy, as if there were a sealed room with no openings in the walls, floor or ceiling. Through the walls (the senses) visitors constantly 'arrive'. Occasionally a visitor (a paranormal perception) comes in through the ceiling. We have no idea of how visitors can arrive through either route. We are, however, so used to their arriving through the walls that we cease to consider it mysterious. The rare visitor through the ceiling, however, arouses in us emotions of amazement and then, when we begin to think about it, we feel that, since there are no openings in the ceiling, such visits are 'paranormal' and impossible. We forget that the same conclusions apply to our everyday, through-the-wall visitors.

The answer of the parapsychologist to the psychologist who demands to know how the paranormally acquired information could possibly have arrived in consciousness must be to apply the same question to the material the psychologist accepts without question in his daily work. Both are equally mysterious. As far as solutions to the problems go, the parapsychologist can legitimately say, 'You show me yours and I'll show you mine.'

> The word 'paranormal', in fact, is not descriptive of events or faculties, but rather of the boundaries that give the Western cultural construct its shape.[11]

During the Second World War a recruit was on guard duty on the outskirts of a training camp on the dusty Kansas plains. A sergeant (like sergeants from time immemorial) was making his life miserable by asking him all sorts of questions about his duty and orders. Finally the sergeant asked, 'What would you do if you saw an enemy battleship coming across the plains towards the camp?' The recruit answered, 'I'd call "up periscope" and torpedo it.' The sergeant asked, 'Where would you get your submarine?' The reply was, 'The same place you got your damn battleship!' The parapsychologist can legitimately demand that the psychologist solve his own 'gap' problem with Type A perceptions before categorically stating that the parapsychologist's 'gap' makes Type B perceptions impossible and invalid.

The biologist E. W. Sinnott wrote: 'How such incompatible things as mind and body can be so closely knit together has been philosophy's perennial despair'.[12] In 1910, the psychologist E. M. Weyer spoke of 'that bridge of cobwebs, closed to science, spanning the chasm between conscious mind and insensate matter'.[13] If one looks at the matter objectively, the mystery of how information 'jumps' from Joe's central nervous system to his consciousness is just as great as the mystery of how the information 'jumps' from Jack's consciousness to Joe's consciousness. In neither case do we know how to deal with the problem. C. E. M. Joad put the situation thus:

> We have not the faintest idea how the transition from event in the brain to experience in consciousness is effected. Hence the fact that there is an unbridgeable gulf in our knowledge of the mode by which what is going on in our mind is communicated to another is not so odd as it might first appear. There is an equally unbridgeable gap in our knowledge of the mode by which what is going on in the body and brain is communicated to the mind that animates them. We forget the mystery of the latter only because it is common; we are astonished by the oddness of the former only because it is rare.[14]

Thus the first real difference we find between Type A and Type B perceptions is in the location of the gap in our knowledge. In Type A it is between our brain and our consciousness. In Type B it is between someone else's consciousness (or the 'target' object) and our consciousness. The mystery in each is just as great. We are, as Joad pointed out, astonished at one and not at the other because of the fact that identified Type A perceptions are common and everyday, and identifiable Type B perceptions are not. The second difference we are able to find is thus in frequency of identifiable occurrence.[15]

If these are the only two differences we can find between Type A and Type B perceptions, why have psychical research and para-psychology languished for so long in the doldrums? Why has progress in the study of the 'paranormal' made so little progress in spite of dedicated and sustained effort by serious, intelligent and well-trained people?

3

THE NEW DEVELOPMENT
IN SCIENCE

Many people, not excluding many scientists, think that science is the business of describing nature more and more accurately, nature being all that is out there in the physical world, independent of ourselves. This is the philosophical position I shall call 'classical realism', and it could hardly be more mistaken: it is utterly, entirely and fundamentally wrong. Science is a process of building mental models representing our experiences. *If the models are useful, and enable us to predict future experiences, then they become the theories of science. If they are not useful they are scrapped. Whether the models seen sensible, or nonsensical, that is, whether we* understand *them or not, is irrelevant.... The models often change radically. Newton's way of looking at the movement of objects like planets, and apples, lasted several hundred years. Then increasing accuracy of measurement in his model representing objects as attracting each other in a certain way showed new problems, and it was replaced by an entirely different one, devised by Einstein, in which objects did not attract each other, they 'distorted the space-time continuum'. Objects moved through this by the easiest path. It is surely not right to suggest that there are certain 'laws of nature' which we aim to discover, or have indeed already discovered. And anything claimed to conflict with them cannot be true. This is indeed the language of the second-rate scientist.* Human experience is pre-eminent. *The question is: Do people have this kind of experience? Can we build a model, a mental construct representing it? The 'laws of nature' are thus temporary useful mental constructs.*[1]

A. J. Ellison

There is a well-known story concerning Einstein's friend, colleague and disciple, Leopold Infeld. Once, prior to the Second

World War, Infeld was asked, 'Is it true that there are only ten people in the world who understand Einstein?' Infeld thought about the matter for several minutes and then replied, 'Oh no. There are at least twenty, but Einstein is not one of them.'

The reason why the implications of the Planck-Einstein revolution have been understood so slowly, and why they were not even fully accepted by Einstein, goes back to an assumption built into Western thinking and incorporated into scientific thought at its very beginning. This assumption is that when we know enough about how the world works, we will find that everything can be explained in essentially the same way. The whole universe and everything in it, this assumption assures us, runs on the same set of laws, the same principles, and when our knowledge is advanced enough we will have proof of this. Whether we are looking at the working of a steam engine or the writing of *Macbeth*, the swimming upstream of a salmon or the cross-channel swim of an athlete, the fall of rain or the dream we had last night, we will find the same system of causes behind them. In the terms of the philosophers, one 'metaphysical system', one 'picture-of-how-the-world-works', will accurately cover them all. It is the task of science to learn more and more about this system of how-things-work and to show how it applies to all the different things that make up the universe.

Put this way the assumption seems so obvious and obviously true that it is hardly worth stating. Yet it is precisely this assumption that the Planck-Einstein revolution of thought showed to be false. Before describing this 'disproof' it is important to see where this assumption came from and why it became such an integral part of our thinking.

Each culture has, at every stage of its development, a body of knowledge regarded as constituting 'common sense'. These are the articles of belief to which, it is commonly assumed, any intelligent person would subscribe. The common-sense beliefs of the place and time of an individual's childhood have a strong tendency to remain within him all his life and to help shape his beliefs about, and reactions to, the events and problems of his later life.

What is true of the development of an individual is also true of the development of a culture. The common sense of the early stages of a new development have a strong tendency to become the basic, often unverbalized, assumptions of the later stages.

When Western society began to develop into our modern culture there was an article of belief that was almost universally regarded as common sense. This was that there was one God, who made the world and everything in it. Catholics, Protestants and Jews (and even our Islamic neighbours) all accepted this, although they differed over theological details.[2]

There is a clear implication to this. If there is one rational God who made the world, He made it in a rational way. One set of laws, 'natural laws', covered everything and there were no exceptions. None. St Augustine had written: 'There is no such thing as a miracle which violates natural law. There are only events which violate our limited knowledge of natural law.' God Himself was bound in His own web of a single definition of 'rationality'.

The world and all its contents, including human beings, could be explained – and could *only* be explained – in a rational way. Even after the concept of the one creator God was no longer accepted, the implication we had drawn from this – that everything in the world could be explained in the same way – remained as a basic assumption in Western thought.[3]

Gradually, the concept of what the one rationality consisted in began to clarify. Since the original great progress of science had been in a particular realm of experience – a realm in which things could be seen and touched – what we learned in that realm deeply influenced our conception of the one rationality. For example, one of the main things we find in the realm where things can be seen and touched, where science made its first great progress, is that things can be separated from each other, added and subtracted. The see-touch realm is a quantitative realm. And so the belief grew up that since part of the universe was quantitative, all of it was quantitative, and a science only advanced as it made its data quantitative. So deep was the belief that we forgot that quantifications – measuring, adding, subtracting – was a human activity imposed on reality. We thought it was part of reality itself. Leibniz's pronouncement 'God is a mathematician' shows this viewpoint very clearly.[4]

Other things peculiar to this see-touch realm were also believed to be part of the basic nature of the universe. For example, one of the things we find in this realm is cause and effect. As long as you are dealing with things that you can see and touch, then all effects have a cause and the effects come after the causes. We did not doubt, and still hardly doubt, that this holds true of the entire universe. With science making great strides in an area where cause and effect always seemed present and obvious, an area of hammers and nails, of cogs and wheels and pulleys, of exploding gun powder and flying cannon balls, it seemed perfectly plain that the universe ran on a specific cause and effect basis: to speak of an uncaused event was ridiculous, as ridiculous as speaking of a cause coming after an event, or of the future influencing the present.

One of the things that inexorably came out of the idea of cause and effect was that if all things run by cause and effect, then the future is predictable. Remember, everything works by cause and effect: the path of the earthworm; the movement of the steam engine; the painting of the Mona Lisa; the light bending in the lens of the telescope; the writing of Beethoven's Ninth Symphony. The future is predictable in principle because each effect follows inevitably from each cause, so that if we know enough about the present we know what causes are operating and therefore what effects will follow. The philosopher Laplace (1749-1827), had the concept of the 'Great Intelligence' that knew the position and velocity of every molecule in the universe. Because he knew this, then he could predict all events for ever and ever in the future. He could also look back to see every event in the past. The physicist Heinz Pagels described this belief clearly:

> From its largest to its smallest motions the entire material creation moves in a way that can be predicted with absolute accuracy by the laws of Newton. Nothing is left to chance. The future is as precisely determined by the past as is the forward movement of a clock.[5]

There is a third basic idea that came from observations made in the see-touch realm and from which generalized assumptions were made about the entire cosmos. It was inevitable that we would develop and accept this idea. Science made great and dramatic progress early in its development in understanding and inventing machines. Since we understood how one part of reality worked and because we believed that *all* of reality works on the same principles, it followed that if you understand anything correctly, you will find that it works on the same principles as a machine.

Machines work on definite principles – things happen when one part pushes or pulls on another (action is by contact and there is no such thing as 'action-at-a-distance'), and so forth; you can *visualize* how a machine works and can make a model of it. The famous nineteenth-century physicist Lord Kelvin wrote: 'I cannot believe any theory until I can make a mechanical model of it.'

This concept – that everything works the way machines work – was again applied generally to the entire universe. Marx saw all society as a great machine running inexorably in its own direction. (About all individual human beings could do to affect it was to so act as to speed it up or slow it down a little.) Freud saw the human personality with a design similar to that of a hydraulic pump and as inexorably *determined*, as absent of free will, as any other machine. (The Behaviourist psychologists saw human beings as being just as mechanical and determined as Freud did, but disagreed with him on the design of the machine.) Darwin saw the evolution of species as being mechanical and determined, although his 'evolution machine' flipped coins in its 'random variations' and then reacted mechanically to the result.[6]

It is no accident that the three great systems of thought developed in the late nineteenth century (Marx, Darwin and Freud) were all based on the mechanical model. We had been so impressed by science's discoveries in the see-touch realm and by our dramatic progress in the development of machines, that we were ready to believe that society, the human mind, the development of species, and everything else, all worked on mechanical principles. As Henry Adams wrote in 1905, the cult of the dynamo had replaced the cult of the Virgin.[7]

This is still the generally held view of Western culture and is essentially where science stood in 1900. There were problems even then – such as the concept of 'fields', which, it was gradually becoming understood, could not be visualized; but overall the position was clear: when our understanding became sufficiently advanced we would see that everything worked on the same basic principles as the steam-engine.

It was in 1900, however, that Max Planck destroyed the validity of this concept for our time. He was working with the problems of sub-atomic particles and discovered that in order to make sense out of his observations he had to devise a new kind of explanatory system, one that differed markedly from the system used to make sense out of observations in the see-touch realm of experience. This was unquestionably one of the greatest scientific discoveries of all time: that for the realm of things too small to be seen or touched – even theoretically – a different explanatory system was needed from that for the realm in which we could see and touch things. As Planck put it, we did not live in a 'one-tracked universe', but in a 'two-tracked' one.[8]

In the science of quantum mechanics – the science Planck devised to make coherent and meaningful observations of the realm of the very small – the entities could not be visualized. An electron is *not* a small, hard, round *(or any other shape)* object moving very fast. It does not have any shape at all. It is a set of numbers. There is no such thing, for example, as an electron standing still. There is no such thing because one of its numbers defines its velocity and without that number it is not an electron, or anything else.

In short, Planck found in this realm of the very small we can neither visualize the entities nor can we make a mechanical model of their actions. This differs fundamentally from the way we organize entities and events in the see-touch realm.

Another aspect of the-way-things-work in the realm of the too-small-to-see-or-touch is that there is no such thing as specific predictability. If there is a mass of radium atoms and the atoms in it keep 'decaying' – emitting particles – then there is no possible way to predict which atom will decay next. We are unable to make this prediction not because we do not know enough, but because *it cannot be done in principle.* No matter how much we knew about the present situation in the radium mass, we could not predict which atom would decay next.

This is because statistical prediction, not specific cause and effect, is what makes things happen in the quantum realm. We can predict precisely *how many* atoms will decay in any period of time, but not *which ones.* 'Cause' simply has a different meaning in the quantum realm than it has in the see-touch realm.[9] The physicist Niels Bohr wrote in this context:

> We are so far removed from a causal description that an atom in a stationary state may in general be said to possess a free choice between possible transitions to other stationary states.[10]

Another difference between these two realms is that all entities of a class are exactly like each other. You cannot find any differences (except position and direction of movement) between one electron and another. The same is true of two protons or two particles of any class. This is not true in other realms of experiences of which we know.[11]

> The old rules held for objects in the everyday world of experience, objects large enough to see and touch, but for the atomic realm below this our ideas have been radically altered. Strange things are true here, and such unexpected concepts are needed to interpret them that the student of physics must learn to think in quite a different way from what he did two generations ago. One of the first things a young physicist must be taught as he enters the laboratory is that 'common sense' will be of little use to him there.[12]

Because of the differences between the two realms we are discussing, the words 'normal' and 'paranormal' ('impossible') apply to different kinds of events in these two realms. It is perfectly normal for an electron to pass through two separate holes in a plate at the same time without splitting. In the see-touch realm this would be 'bilocation', a distinctly paranormal event. An electron may go from one path ('orbit') to another without ever being in or crossing the space between. If you or I did this, it would be tele-portation and the Society for Psychical Research would certainly want to study us.

For example, it would be *very* paranormal for a medium to do the following things:

1. Tell where an electron is and how fast it is going.

2. In a mass of radium atoms that are decaying – emitting particles – tell which atom is going to emit a particle next.

3. Tell if an event on the star Vega and an event in this room happened at the same time.

As we shall see later, if 'paranormal' and 'normal' apply to different kinds of events in different realms, it is important to ask *in which realms we observe phenomena such as telepathy.* We shall then have to ask if the term 'paranormal' applies to telepathy in the realms in which it is observed.

Planck, then, showed that we live in a 'two-tracked universe'. A few years later, Einstein showed that we need a third 'track', a new metaphysical system, to make sense of what we observe in a third realm of experience – the realm of things too big or too fast for us to see or touch, even theoretically. In this realm of the very-big-and-fast, things are again very different from the realm accessible to the senses. For example, here there are no such concepts as 'space' or 'time'. These blend together and simply *cannot* be dealt with separately. Here also – as in the realm of the very small – things normally happen that would be impossible in the see-touch realm. If two events occur, for example, it is often impossible to ask 'Which event occurred first, or did they occur at the same time?' The question often has no meaning.[13]

For additional examples of the 'strangeness' of this realm of experience, we might look at the fact that the faster an object in it moves (relative to us), the larger it gets, the shorter it gets and the slower run the wrist watches of anyone riding on it. These are highly paranormal occurrences in the see-touch realm, but perfectly normal in the realm of the very-big-and-fast.

In spite, however, of his deep and profound understanding, Einstein was also a man of his time and his society. He believed that there was ultimately only *one* explanation to the question of how-the-universe-works, and that the different explanatory systems we are now forced to use would yield to one system when we understood more. He believed that the different metaphysical systems, the different kinds of explanations, we must use in different realms were temporary expedients; that we would eventually be able to abandon them in favour of the one explanatory system that fits the entire cosmos. It was for this reason that he rejected the idea that there is no such thing as cause and effect in the quantum universe, the realm of the very small, and that the explanatory system which fits this realm is that of statistical causation. That is why he made his famous statement: 'I cannot believe that God plays dice with the universe.' This statement shows both why Einstein rejected the new work in quantum mechanics (a field which he helped start, and for which he received the Nobel Prize) and the origin of his belief that there is only one valid explanatory system for the entire universe.

Very early in its history, the Church split into three groups on this fundamental philosophical question: 'Is there more than one valid explanatory system?' The matter at immediate issue concerned the way to deal with information derived from faith and revelation on the one hand and information from the senses on the other. The basic issue, however, concerned the number of valid explanatory systems. The first group followed Tertullian. They held that revelation alone uncovers truth; philosophy and the senses only deceive. The study of the world by means of the senses and reason is heretical. There is only one true explanatory system, and that is given by faith.

The second group, following St Augustine, Origen and Clement of Alexandria, believed that revelation is the only possible starting point for all valid knowledge, including that of the physical world. It, and only it, leads to reason and scientific truth. As St Augustine put it: 'Understanding is the reward of faith. Therefore, seek not to understand that thou mayest believe, but believe that thou mayest understand.' Faith and reason, from this viewpoint, if applied correctly, always give the same answers.

The third group, led by Averroes, believed that faith and reason can disagree, but both can still be valid. In other words, there can be different explanatory systems, each valid for its own realm of experience. They believed that philosophers and theologians should each respect the different viewpoint of the other. This was the Doctrine of the Double Truth, the doctrine of Siger of Brabant, who debated with Thomas Aquinas on the subject. The official decision was in favour of Aquinas, and the Augustinian point of view. As far as the Church was concerned the matter was closed. It is interesting to speculate how different our cultural heritage might have been if the decision had gone the other way.

How close modern science has come to the rejected third viewpoint – that different metaphysical systems are necessary and lead to different results – can be shown in a quotation from Arthur S. Eddington, one of the greatest of our modern physicist-philosophers.

In my observatory there is a telescope which condenses the light of a star on a film of sodium in a photo-electric cell. I rely on the classical theory to conduct the light through the lenses and focus it on the cell: then I switch on to the quantum theory to make the light fetch out electrons from the sodium film to be collected in an electrometer. If I happen to transpose the two theories, the quantum theory convinces me that the light will never get concentrated in the cell, and the classical theory shows that it is powerless to extract the electrons if it does get in. I have no logical reason for not using the theories this way round, only experience teaches me that I must not. Sir William Bragg was correct when he said that we use Classical Theory on Mondays, Wednesdays and Fridays, and the Quantum Theory on Tuesdays, Thursdays and Saturdays.[14]

At the very beginning of modern science, Francis Bacon had warned us against the trap (the Idols of the Tribe) of finding more regularity and order in the world than is really there. Celestial bodies do not move in perfect circles as we once assumed, and there is no one way of looking at everything that is valid for them all. Bacon put the twentieth-century viewpoint clearly when he wrote that all systems of thought were: 'so many strange plays representing worlds of men's creations after an unreal and scenic fashion.' Or, as Charles Fort put it: 'I can conceive of nothing in philosophy, science, or religion that is more than the proper costume to wear for a time.'

The first of the Sceptics, Pyrrho of Elis (c. 270 BC) thought that we perceive things, not as they are, but as they appear in accidental relations to each other and to ourselves. Further, he pointed out that untrustworthy senses and untrustworthy reason cannot combine to give us any absolute knowledge of reality. It has taken a long time for science to come back to this viewpoint.

A number of papers in the literature of parapsychology have discussed the relationships between modern field-theory, the study of consciousness, and such problems as 'survival'. These frequently brilliant papers (e.g.,[15, 16]) and their implications could not be taken seriously or followed up by the scientific establishment because of the unverbalized assumption that there was *really* only one valid way to comprehend the entire cosmos.

We had, early in the century, a three-tracked universe: the realm of the very small, the sensory realm (the realm accessible to sight and touch), and the realm of the very large or fast. How many do we have today? How many different metaphysical systems does science need to deal with our experience?

How many will be needed in the future is impossible to say. Today we find we need five.

In addition to the three described above, we find we need another to describe and deal with meaningful human behaviour, and yet another to deal with our own consciousness. I shall be discussing these realms in some detail because *it is in these realms*

that we observe meaningful Type B perceptions — telepathy and the like.
We will find that the metaphysical systems needed to explain our
observations in these two realms are as different from the one that
is useful and necessary in the see-touch realm as are the world-
pictures needed to explain our observations of the realm of the very
small or the realm of the very large and fast. For example, there is
no such thing as 'space' in the realm of consciousness, and there are
at least four different kinds of space (in each of which we behave
differently) in the realm of meaningful behaviour.

It is important to be clear that each realm of experience needs *a
different metaphysical system* to make the data from it coherent, to
make our observations meaningful. These systems are very
different — the definitions of 'space', 'time', 'causality', 'observer',
'experiment', 'normal' and 'paranormal' are often different in
different realms. Different the systems are; contradictory they are
not. Data from one realm does not make data from another realm
impossible. There is a compatibility among valid metaphysical
systems, *'Weltbilds'*, pictures-of-how-the-world-works, even
though they vary considerably from each other.

This concept is a difficult one to grasp. We have learned so well
through centuries of cultural development that common sense
(which Einstein once called 'that collection of prejudices accumulated by age 18') will serve us in all realms of experience — that it
reflects the one basic truth of the universe — that it is hard to realize
what a limited guide it is. It is a good and necessary guide for the
see-touch realm, but not for others. Common sense boggles at
truths from other realms, for instance:

at the fact that there are as many points on a line one inch long
as there are points on a line one mile long;

at the fact that there are just as many odd numbers as there are
odd and even numbers combined;

at the fact that the universe is finite (limited in size), but
unbounded;

that for certain events there is no probability of their
occurring before they happen (the probability is not 0 per
cent or 50 per cent or 100 per cent or anything else). After
they have happened the probability is 100 per cent;

that there are certain things that you cannot dismantle into their basic components and then put together and have them function as well as before;

that 'space' has many different meanings and that each of them has equal validity: the 'correct' definition depends on what you are trying to do;

that between the stars and between the galaxies there is no such thing as empty space in the sense we consider a vase or jar to contain empty space. A light ray travelling from one star to another is not moving in empty space but in fields of force that will eventually bring it back to where it started.

These examples strain our minds. Yet a specialist in any of the areas concerned will attest to their truth.

It would be easy to give many more examples. These will suffice, however, to make the point that 'common sense', the rule of the see-touch realm, is no longer the clear guide it was once in science. Common sense means different things in different realms of experience.

To sum up. Science today starts by choosing a *domain* of experience to study. We might choose the domain of non-organic chemical reactions, night observations of the sky, or wind, cloud, and weather changes, or of a flat, two-dimensional universe. The last, for example, would yield to our study such observables as lines, angles, distances, shapes. We would study the relationships between them. As we came to understand more and more about these relationships we would develop the science of Plane Geometry. We would ask what definitions of 'space', 'time', 'causality' and so on (the 'guiding principles') we needed in this domain to make our data coherent. We would believe that when we found the correct definitions, all the observables in this domain would be lawfully related to each other. When we found the correct definitions, we would consider that this domain was in the same *realm* as all other domains that used the same definitions of the guiding principles. Plane geometry, for example, would be in the Sensory Realm, in which the definitions are those given us by the senses, particularly those of vision and touch. We would find that the laws we developed in Plane Geometry that related the observables were coherent with laws developed in other domains.

Further, we would find that what we learned about the Sensory Realm would be compatible, though often very different, with what we learned in other realms, such as the Quantum Realm (the realm of the too-small-to-see-or-touch, even theoretically) or the Relativity Realm (the realm of the too-big-or-fast-to-see-or-touch, even theoretically).

This is the basis of the revolution in science that, on the whole, has been neither accepted nor understood in parapsychology. With a few exceptions, parapsychologists have tried to build their explanatory theories on the 'one-tracked universe' model of eighteenth- and nineteenth-century science rather than the 'multi-tracked universe' model of the twentieth. They have not accepted William James's dictum that we no longer live in a 'universe', but in a 'pluriverse'. As the parapsychologist Steve Rosen has put it: 'Whatever the particular model of parascientific phenomena has been, it has been cast in the epistemological model of the old science.'[17] In his important paper, Rosen goes on to suggest that parapsychology badly needs a major programme of 'epistemotherapy'.

However, if we accept the concept that there are different realms of experience (each with its own definition of 'space', 'causality', and so forth) it becomes necessary to ask in which realm we observe Type B perceptions. We find that we observe them in the realm of consciousness and the realm of meaningful behaviour.

In her extensive analysis of 'spontaneous' cases,[18] Louisa Rhine has pointed out that these psi occurrences manifest themselves in intuitions, dreams and hallucinations. These are phenomena of the Realm of Consciousness. We can evaluate them as phenomena of this realm. We can also evaluate them as phenomena of the Realm of Meaningful Behaviour in terms of what the person *does* as a result of them – writes a letter to the Society for Psychical Research, tells others, records it in a diary, goes for a walk to clear his head, takes a sedative, etc. These are the only two realms in which we observe the phenomena. Others in the field have also made this clear. Ian Stevenson, in his *Telepathic Impressions,*[19] analyzes this carefully, whilst W. A. H. Rushton, a President of the Society for Psychical Research, wrote:

Both [Type A and Type B perceptions] may give fairly reliable information about affairs in the outside world at a distance, and this information comes not like a set of scientific measurements from which answers may be calculated, it springs immediately and miraculously into consciousness whole and clear, and without more ado we see what we see.[20]

This fact – that Type B perceptions are observed in the Realm of Consciousness and the Realm of Meaningful Behaviour – changes our perception of them, and of the problems they imply, to a considerable degree. If, for example, as the philosopher, A. J. Ayer put it, 'the mind has no position in space – it is by definition not the sort of thing that can have a position in space',[21] why have we consistently seen the problem of telepathy (Type B perception) as the problem of how the information travelled from the *position* of one mind to the *position* of another? This is the sort of unsolvable, headache-causing problem we raise when we try to solve the problems arising from our observations in one realm of experience with the explanatory system of another. I shall explore this problem as it applies to parapsychology in detail in the following chapters.[22]

4

THE REALM OF CONSCIOUSNESS

It is when life is associated with consciousness that we reach different ground altogether. To those who have any intimate acquaintance with the laws of chemistry and physics, the suggestion that the . . . world [of consciousness] could be ruled by laws of allied character is as preposterous as the suggestion that a nation could be ruled by laws like the laws of grammar.[1]

A. S. Eddington

As has been pointed out in the previous chapter, paranormal occurrences are observed in two realms of experience. These are the Realm of Consciousness and the Realm of Meaningful Behaviour. In the next three chapters, I plan to examine psi in each of these two realms, starting with the Realm of Consciousness. As E. B. Titchener wrote in the book that established scientific psychology in America, 'Psychology springs from the question: What is the difference between oneself and the things outside oneself?'[2]

In the medieval period, one of the strangest aspects of consciousness was first understood. It was called 'Intentional Inexistence' by the scholastic philosophers of the time, and it referred to the fact that our consciousness is generally far less aware of itself than it is of the objects we perceive. We perceive a world of objects and stimuli: we then focus on them and their perceived attributes. Attention is on them and their relationships, not on our consciousness itself. In effect, as the Scholastics put it, consciousness *disappears* into its objects; or as William James wrote: 'Thought always appears to deal with objects independent of itself.'

The art theorist Roger Fry pointed to a similar phenomenon in the field of painting which may help to make this more comprehensible. A good painting, wrote Fry, is 'a glass and a transparency'. When we look at it we are not aware of the painting, but of its subject. Similarly, consciousness is a glass and a transparency; it disappears into the objects it perceives: 'The understanding, like the eye, while it makes us see and perceive all other things, takes no notice of itself; and it requires art and pains to set it at a distance and make it its own object.'[3]

This has been known for a long time. It has, however, never to my knowledge been applied to the problems of parapsychology. In this chapter, I plan to attempt to begin this application.

We define consciousness as that realm which is composed of our inner experience. It includes the non-physical observables which we are aware are 'inside' of us rather than 'outside'. It is the realm of experience of our own, non-physical activity.

I shall be exploring some of the ways in which the data from, and the guiding principles of this realm (such as definitions of space, time and causality) differ from those of the world accessible to the senses – the world of things we can see or touch. First it is appropriate to demonstrate that we all *know* there is a real difference between the two, that we *know* consciousness cannot be explained by, or reduced to, those laws and principles we use so successfully to explain how machines or computers, or anything accessible to our senses, work. We will do this by means of a simple thought experiment.[4]

You are deeply in love with Suzy. She dies and I offer you a substitute – Sally – a perfect robot who will look and feel and act exactly as Suzy did. In short, a computerized replica that is so perfect that if you were not aware of the substitution, there would be no clues in its actions or anything you could detect with your senses that would tell you it was not Suzy. Sally will stay with you the rest of your life, growing older exactly as Suzy would have. Would you accept my offer?

It would be a most unusual person who *would* accept such a substitution. Most of us would feel a repulsion at the idea. We might conceive that it was possible we would fall in love with Suzy's sister Sarah, but not with Sally. Even the most thoroughgoing reductionist – one who believes that all human activity can be reduced to, and explained by, the same principles that govern the actions of a machine or a computer – would be extremely unlikely to accept the substitution. And yet this seems unreasonable. After all, if Suzy was, in essence, the same kind of entity that a machine is, if everything she did or said was determined in the same way; in short, if she was really nothing but a soft-skinned and pleasantly curved machine, then what would be the real difference between her and Sally? There would be none from this viewpoint. You might just as well marry one as the other.

But we all *know* that this is not so. We all know that we are not machines and neither are those we love. We know that our bodies may well work on the same principles as a machine does, but our inner life is something different. We know that our real self – our hopes, fears, dreams, joys and loves – are not computer productions or artefacts. In short, we know that our consciousness is something 'other', something different. We loved Suzy not for the parts of her that followed the principles of a machine, but for the parts of her that didn't. And further, we loved her with the non-machine-like parts of ourself. (We might go even farther and say that the healthiest parts of our consciousness are the least computer-like and the unhealthiest parts the most. Thus in those areas where we are the least free because of our neurotic binding, we react in the most predictable and machine-like way.)

If our consciousness does not work on the same principles as things we can see and touch, on what principles does it work? What sort of system will explain what goes on in our inner life if the common-sense, everyday one does not apply? A central theme of the previous chapters has been that, from the viewpoint of modern science, there is no one correct way of describing how everything in the universe works. There are a number of different explanations, each proper, necessary and useful for certain parts of reality. As Cyril Burt put it: 'Unlike the Victorian physicist, we no longer believe that Nature, in constructing the universe or in keeping it going, is bound by the same simple principles as a human engineer.'[5]

The drive towards simplicity, towards the single elegant explanation of everything that is, the drive that characterized the science and philosophy of the last three centuries, collapsed with the publication of Max Planck's development of quantum mechanics in 1900. The implications of this collapse are only now beginning to be understood in physics and other sciences. To put the new insight as succinctly as possible, we now understand that you cannot explain the attraction a Rembrandt painting has for us in the same terms, with the same explanatory system, that you use to explain the chemistry of the paint the artist used. Or, in the example used by the physicist Arthur Eddington, you cannot analyze the likeableness of an elephant with the same system you use to analyze its ponderosity.

Psi-events are events in consciousness. Therefore, if we wish to explain and understand them, we must use the system of explanation applicable to this realm. We cannot use the common-sense, everyday explanation we use to explain bicycles and steam engines. Attempting to explain how observables act in one realm with the metaphysical system of another can lead to headaches, but not to progress.

Phenomena in the Sensory Realm can be described in visual terms. In an elaborate analogy, in which he compared the individual mind to the city of Rome, Freud showed that it: 'leads to the inconceivable, or even to absurdities, to try to master the idiosyncrasies of mental life ... by treating them in terms of visual representation. . . . It is impossible to represent [conscious] phenomena ... in visual terms.'[6]

In order to begin to understand what system of description and explanation is needed for the realm of consciousness, let us start by asking: What do we observe in this realm?

To our surprise, the first thing we see is that there are no 'things' in this realm, only processes. Titchener wrote: 'whenever we look inward, we find nothing but processes'.

> A 'thing' is permanent, relatively unchanging, definitely marked off from other 'things'. A process is, by etymology, a 'moving forward'. . . . [The] psychology [of consciousness] deals always with *processes* and never with things.[7]

It is not just that I observe only processes in consciousness; my consciousness itself is in the form of a process. It is one flowing, an ever-becoming 'river', with no real demarcation points. Even after the gaps of sleep or unconsciousness, it is the same consciousness, belonging to me and not to a different consciousness. Each moment of consciousness is a part of the continuing stream to the same degree – and can be isolated only in the same arbitrary way – as each foot of the river is a part of the on-flowing stream. Further, no matter how sharply we isolate a moment of consciousness, we find that it is a unity synthesized out of its many aspects which cannot be meaningfully subdivided as can things in the realm accessible to the senses. An idea of half a book is reasonable. Half of an idea of a book is not.[8]

In Sherrington's words, the recognition of our own consciousness is in terms of a process, not a thing or a collection of individual bits. The 'enchanted loom' weaves 'a dissolving pattern, always a meaningful pattern, though never an abiding one; a shifting harmony of subpatterns'.[9] The point was perhaps first made by Descartes when he wrote that the body is divisible but the mind is not.

Part of the problem of comprehending the dynamic flowing of consciousness, and how this differs from the individuality of things and their bumpings and interactions in the sensory realm, is that our language itself is designed on the basis of the observations we have made in the sensory realm. This language structure then reinforces our idea that everything, including consciousness, has the same structure as the language we use to describe it. This is a far cry from the viewpoint of modern science. C. K. Ogden put the matter in this way:

> All current languages embody in their grammar and vocabulary an outlook upon the world which is passing away. The fact that we are forced to use nouns for what are essentially happenings rather than things (as when we say 'an emotion', 'a perception', 'a thought' instead of an emotional, a perceptive, or a ratiocinative event) is an example. The struggle which psychology is now having to rid itself of a false 'atomism', to arrive at 'dynamic' conceptions is primarily a struggle against a bad legacy in language.[10]

(One is reminded of Wittgenstein's 'All philosophy is a struggle against the bedevilment of language'.)

Let us continue our exploration of our inner world. As we do, another difference from the world of experience accessible to the senses immediately appears. It is that access to consciousness is private rather than public. 'It is obvious,' wrote the psychologist Franz Brentano, 'that no mental phenomena can be perceived by more than one person.'[11] We have, on the contrary, public access to observables, data, in the sensory realm. You and I can agree or disagree on the length of a table. We can measure it and come to an agreement as to how long it is. We can even agree on what method to use to solve our disagreement if there is one – a yardstick, or a pulse of coherent light, or the decision of an 'objective' observer. But only I can observe the processes in my own consciousness. We cannot disagree about whether or not I feel sad. We can find no way for you to observe my sadness and an 'objective observer' is a meaningless term here. Where would we find him and what would he do? Hugo Munsterberg, in 1899, regarded this as one of the central facts of psychology. He defined 'physical' as 'all that is a possible object for every subject', and 'psychical' as 'all that is a possible object for one subject only'.[12]

It is partly for this reason that events in consciousness are, *in principle,* non-quantifiable. If I cannot observe your joy and you cannot observe mine, then how can we ever agree on how much joy constitutes one 'exuberant'? And if I say that I have two 'dols' of pain in my toothache, how can you ever know how much pain that signifies? 'Now it is the essence of mental things,' wrote the philosopher Henri Bergson, 'that they do not lend themselves to measurement.'[13]

> You cannot have a ton of love (in spite of the way girls used to sign their letters) or a yard of hate or a gallon of numinous awe; but love and hate and awe are just as real as a ton of flour or a yard of linen or a gallon of petrol, more real indeed, because they have immediate significance, they are not simply means to ends like making bread, a pillow case or haste.[14]

The famous nineteenth-century axiom, 'Whatever exists, exists in some quantity', may well be true, but in the Realm of Consciousness this 'quantity' is not the type that can be numbered, added, subtracted, divided or multiplied. I may describe a particular feeling I have today as 'more' or 'much more', 'less' or 'much less' than a similar feeling I had yesterday; but that is about all I can do.[15] 'It is the mark of a properly trained mind to look for a degree of precision that is appropriate to the subject matter, and only to the degree that the nature of each allows,' wrote Aristotle in his *Nicomachean Ethics.*

We can, of course, measure how much action an emotion leads to. This, however, does not quantify our feeling, but our response to it. These are fundamentally different things and the feeling itself is only one factor among many that determines the response. If, in the words of the old cigarette advertisement, I walk a mile for a Camel, it is not only my feeling of desire for a cigarette that determines whether or not I set out on the hike: it is also my general feelings of strength or fatigue, whether or not I enjoy walking, my other plans for the next hour, and whether or not I have read the latest report on smoking and lung cancer. If I walk one mile for a cigarette and you walk two miles, this does not mean that your desire (or addiction) is twice as great as mine, but only that your response is. Not only might you feel the need for exercise more than I; I might not like giving in to my own desires as much as you. Besides, my feet might hurt.

Another finding as we explore the Realm of Consciousness is that the situation is always changing and never repeats itself. *'No state of consciousness,'* wrote William James, *'once gone, can recur and be identical with what it was before...'* [italics his].[16] James continues: 'A permanently existing idea... which makes its appearance before the flashlight of consciousness at periodic intervals is as mythical as the Jack of Spades.'[17]

This concept that the situation never repeats itself seems surprising and unlikely at first, accustomed as we are to the model of the physical sciences (created and appropriate for the realm of experience accessible to the senses) by means of which a situation can be recreated and an experiment repeated. I can make a repeatable experiment in these fields because I can *isolate* a specific system of interesting events and recreate this system again and again in the same manner. There are, however, a number of fields in which this cannot be done. As Henri Bergson put it:

> History does not repeat itself. The battle of Austerlitz was fought once and it will never be fought again. It being impossible that the same historical conditions should ever be reproduced, the same historical fact cannot be repeated: and as a law expresses necessarily that to certain causes, always the same, there will correspond an effect, also always the same, history strictly speaking has no bearing on laws, but on particular facts, and on the no less particular circumstances which brought them to pass.[18]

In a fascinating essay, Søren Kierkegaard attempted to find an example of exact repetition in life. Search as he could through places he had lived in before, he could not find one. His conclusion: 'There is no such thing as repetition.'[19]

What is true in the realm in which history is studied is as true in the realm of consciousness. This is one reason that it is not possible, in principle, to produce a repeatable experiment in parapsychology any more than it is in history. Even if a parapsychological experiment is repeated by the same scientist he – as the parapsychologist Robert Brier has pointed out[20] – is doing it for the second time. If it is done by a different scientist, there is also a major difference. (The same problem applies to the subjects in the experiments.) The question of repeatability in science is not one of exact repetition, but of which differences make a difference. In certain fields – as in chemistry – the difference between experimenters – whether, for instance, the experimenter is a virgin – in terms of *this* experiment does not make a difference. In fields involving consciousness, however, they make a real difference. In certain fields, repeatability of experiments is a possible and a useful criterion of method. In other fields it is neither a useful concept nor a possible procedure.

> One of the cornerstones of scientific methodology is the formula *ceteris paribus* – 'other things being equal'. But other things are never equal where human subjects are concerned... ask any writer, painter or scientist to define the precise conditions under which the creative spark will repeatedly and predictably ignite the vapours in his mind! and creativity is a less elusive and mysterious faculty than psi....[21]

A 'repeatable experiment' in the realm of consciousness tells us we are dealing with a damaged person. If, in a free-association test, every time we give the word 'black' the subject replies 'white', and we can repeat this indefinitely (without ever getting a response like 'boring', for example), we know that something is wrong. We know that this person is so damaged that his response pattern is frozen, that he is so emotionally tied up or so heavily conditioned that the natural response is no longer present.

An artist who, standing in the same spot at the same time of day, painted exactly the same picture over and over again would be regarded as an extremely damaged person. We would expect a camera to exactly reproduce the same thing under the same conditions, but not an artist. If, for example, we look at the repeated paintings by Van Gogh of the wheat fields at Arles, or at Cezanne's repeated paintings of Mont Sainte-Victoire, we see that each one is a completely distinct and very different painting. There is no repetition. At any one of the times that Van Gogh or Cezanne set up their easel, it would have been impossible in principle to predict what the new painting was going to look like.

For real individual human beings we cannot predict what is going to happen in their consciousness or what their molar behaviour will be. We can no more predict what the next novel of a writer will be on the basis of his previous novels than we could have predicted what the Ninth Symphony would be like after hearing its eight forerunners. (We would, for example, be certain that there would be no voices in it.) Human beings are non-predictable in principle. Only papier mâché characters can be predicted. We can make 100 per cent accurate predictions that Tom Swift, Tarzan, and James Bond will emerge triumphant from their next adventure. Not so for Captain Cook, Al Capone or Albert Einsten.

A prediction about molar human behaviour, or conscious activity, is a prediction about a single event. Such an event can never be repeated since the conditions that are important can never be exactly the same. As T. R. Sarbin has shown so clearly, such a prediction, if made, is non-verifiable (or non-falsifiable) in principle. If I say that the chances are one in six that Jones will commit suicide within a year, how is such a statement to be confirmed or shown to be false? If Jones commits suicide (or if he does not) the result is equally compatible with my statement, with the statement 'The chances are one in two that Jones will commit suicide within a year', or with the statement that the chances are one in ten. Probability statements about a single event are non-verifiable.[22]

This applies to statistical predictions. The problem is the same when we attempt to make absolute predictions in the realm of molar behaviour or in the Realm of Consciousness. An absolute prediction needs a general law and no laws can be made when the situation cannot be repeated with the important variables held constant. This cannot be done in these realms. With no absolute laws (i.e., Boyle's Law) we cannot make absolute predictions. In the words of the founder of Experimental Psychology, Wilhelm Wundt: 'There is no psychological law to which the exceptions are not more numerous than the agreements.'

In the realm of large numbers of people I *can* make statistical predictions. From what I know of present social conditions and engineers, I predict that at the next annual convention of the American Association of Electrical Engineers between 36 and 42 per cent will wear ties to meetings in the morning. This prediction I can check out. But I cannot predict in the realm of specific individuals, and if I do, my predictions only *sound* as if they had any meaning. There is no way that I can check them. If I say that there is a 40 per cent chance that the twenty-first engineer who comes into the registration hall on Tuesday morning will be wearing a tie, am I actually saying *anything?* I stand at the entrance to the hall, let twenty engineers pass and look at the twenty-first, an engineer named Ralph Stone. He is wearing a tie. Is my prediction borne out? It is impossible to tell. I can make a guess as to whether Stone will be wearing a tie or not, and I can be correct or not. But there are no laws by means of which I can make an absolute prediction. And a statistical prediction has no meaning in this realm.

The molar behaviour of groups of individuals is in a different realm of experience than the molar behaviour of one person. This is demonstrated by the successful prediction of actuarial statistics versus the impossibility of predicting the behaviour of any one individual. As quantum mechanics have demonstrated, there is no paradox involved here. In different realms, different things are possible and different things are impossible. With one particle or person I can, at best, make a pretty fair guesstimate: with large numbers of either, I can predict with very great accuracy.

In a chemistry (or any other domain in the sensory realm) experiment, if absolute repeatability does *not* occur (i.e., if the match does not light the magnesium strip each time), we know that something is very wrong. In the realm of consciousness, if absolute repeatability *does* occur, we know that something is very wrong.

Further, the essence of a repeatable experiment is that the collection of events you are studying be isolated from everything else, so that you can see that they are affecting each other and not being affected by random stimuli in the environment. If I want to study the effect of barbiturates on the brain waves of a white rat, I have to make sure that my brainwave (EEG) machine is picking up only the brain waves. I have to shield out the electrical effects of the light bulbs in the ceiling (many an early EEG experimental protocol reported rats and people having 60 cycles per second brain waves, particularly at night), the electrical discharges of the lift going past my floor, and perhaps even the ocean waves pounding on a nearby beach. If I want to study the effect of drugs on the behaviour of animals, I must also isolate my animals from temperature changes, food changes, and the introduction of an attractive member of the same species, but of the opposite sex, into a nearby cage. This is clearly understood by scientists. But how do I set up an isolation situation when I am studying an ability that is influenced by the mood and personality of anyone else involved, goes through walls as if they weren't there, isn't even blocked by the curve of the earth over thousands of miles, can even sometimes violate the time barrier, and brings us information of events that have not even happened yet? How do I screen out the attitudes, personality and parapsychological abilities of the experimenter, the laboratory assistant, someone in the nearby corridors, or a person interested in this particular problem who is 7000 miles away? Is the experimenter using precognition to select just those random numbers which the subject will later guess? Are the subjects actually picking up the target pictures by telepathy, or are the judges saying that they are because the judges are using clairvoyance to determine which is the correct card? Who is doing what to whom? One famous psychical researcher, G. N. M. Tyrrell, said a typical parapsychology experiment was set up on the following model. There is a large room, in the centre of which is an open safe full of money. At night, thirty people sleep in the room. They have all been selected for the same reason − they are all sleepwalkers. In the morning, the money is still in the safe. What happened during the night?

You cannot isolate the important variables in a parapsychological system. For this reason, as well as for others we shall come to presently, the idea of a repeatable experiment in parapsychology is beyond attainment. This, as we have established, is also true for any research in the field of consciousness, as well as for the field of human history.

One difference between the sensory realm and the realm of consciousness that is rarely described is the difference between the tendency to keep 'things' constant and the tendency to keep 'relationships' constant. In the sensory realm, things tend to stay what they are. A rock has a strong tendency to remain a rock, whether or not its location and surrounding temperature are changed and whether or not it is moved, with or without accompanying music, from strong sunlight to the bottom of a lake. In this realm, relationships between things tend to vary much more easily than the things themselves.

In the realm of consciousness, there are no 'things' but the relationships between the various aspects of the process we call consciousness show a strong tendency to remain constant. Thus we tend to feel a certain way in the presence of a certain kind of perception once the connection has been made. Each time that kind of perception is made the same kind of feeling tone tends to follow or accompany it. As Josiah Royce put it, 'Couplings in the mind – relationships – have a curious stubbornness.'[23] Every psychotherapist knows how hard it is to break such a relationship in a phobia, an erotic attachment or an obsession. One might say that generally the 'homoeostatic' forces in the sensory realm apply to *things*;.in the realm of consciousness they apply to *relationships.*

As we continue our exploration of the Realm of Consciousness, we find that the methods of logic and of mathematics, which have proven so useful in our understanding of the Realm of Sensory Experience, cannot be used here. They simply do not apply.

This is due not only to the fact that we cannot find 'things' in consciousness that can be separated from each other and whose effects on each other could be studied, nor to the fact that we cannot quantify the observables (variables) we find in consciousness and so cannot add, subtract, multiply or divide them. It is also because one of the basic laws of the sensory realm does not apply in the Realm of Consciousness. This is the Law of Contradiction. In the Realm of Sensory Experience a thing cannot be both 'A' and 'Not-A' at the same time. It is either 'A' or it isn't. You cannot be travelling East and not-East at a particular moment. This is a fundamental law of sensory reality and enables us to use our logic and mathematics so well and effectively in this realm.

In the Realm of Consciousness, this is simply not true. I can believe and not believe something at the same time and with no particular difficulty. I can be heartbroken at the death of a character in my favourite soap opera and send (as many people do) flowers to the funeral, and see nothing insane in sending the flowers to a television station rather than to the mythical town where the characters regularly pretend to interact. I can weep as Mimi dies in *La Bohème*; or I can be on the edge of my seat, tense with the possibilities of what may happen, desperately hoping Iago won't get away with his deceptions as I watch *Othello* for the eighth time. I can love someone and – at the same moment – be so full of rage against her that my blood-pressure goes up a dozen points.

(Indeed, this is pointed out in the rather hysterical note so frequently heard in the voices of those who loudly announce that paranormal occurrences do not occur. As Cyril Burt has somewhere remarked, they remind one of the village girl who said, in one of Conan Doyle's stories, 'We don't believe in ghosts, but we 'um horribly afraid of them.' This is often expressed in novel and ingenious ways. One well-known psychiatrist read a paper by Jules Eisenbud on telepathy. He then told Eisenbud: 'Chance coincidences occur far more often than the laws of probability would lead one to believe.'[24])

This difference between the Realm of Sensory Experience and the Realm of Consciousness was first made clear in the seventeenth century by Pascal, the great philosopher and mathematician who invented the geometry of conic sections at sixteen years of age. He distinguished between those realms of experience which could be analyzed by the 'geometric spirit', and those that must be analyzed by the 'subtle spirit'. The geometric spirit, he said, is valid for those realms that can be analyzed into individual components. Where this analysis cannot be made, we need a different method – the 'subtle spirit'.[25] As A. S. Eddington put it:

> Natural law is not applicable to the unseen world behind the symbolism because it is unadapted to anything except symbols and its perfection is a perfection of symbolic linking. You cannot apply such a scheme to parts of our personality which are not measurable by symbols any more than we can extract the square root of a sonnet.[26]

With such a fundamental law as the principle of contradiction not relevant to the Realm of Consciousness, it is clear that our usual, common-sense methods of logic and mathematics are not relevant either.

Another factor that clearly differentiates the Realm of Consciousness from the Realm of Sensory Experience is that in the former, anything that is examined is changed by the examination. If we are angry at someone and, being curious about the nature of our consciousness, carefully examine how it feels to be angry, we shortly find that our feelings are now very different. The very analysis of the emotion has changed it. This is also true of other emotions. If someone says sincerely that they love you, do not ask 'Why?' It is an irrelevant question and if the person pays too much attention to it and really starts analyzing the emotion, its attributes and sources, you are likely to wind up nothing more than good friends. In the words of e. e. cummings:

> Since feeling is first
> who pays any attention
> to the syntax of things
> will never wholly kiss you.[27]

What I have tried to do in this chapter is simply to point out some of the ways that the Realm of Consciousness differs from the Realm of Sensory Experience, and show that a completely different system of explanation must be used in relation to it. In this new system of explanation, the one that is valid in one realm in which paranormal events are observed, there is nothing we know of that forbids their existence. In the Realm of Consciousness, paranormal events are as normal and reasonable as anything else that goes on. It is because we have been looking for their explanation in the wrong place – in the Sensory Realm – that there has seemed to be such an impossible paradox.[28]

Before leaving this exploration of the Realm of Consciousness, however, there are three special aspects to be noted. These three have especially important implications for the problem of the paranormal. They are the concepts of 'space', of 'purpose', and of 'causation'.

The concept of space may differ considerably in different realms of experience. As mentioned earlier, one of the things we have learned in this century, for example, is that in the realm in which things are too large or going by too fast to be accessible to the senses, space simply does not exist as a guiding principle in its own right. We can only observe and deal with it after it has been inextricably merged with time into the guiding principle 'space-time'.

What is the meaning of the term 'space' in the Realm of Consciousness? As we look within we find that the term seems to have no meaning here. The philosopher Immanuel Kant wrote in the seventeenth century that space was a form we apply to the world of outside things, time a form that we apply to the inner world. Indeed, space does seem primarily to apply to the realm of things we can see and touch. When we look within, however, we cannot find the spatial relationships of the observables. I am interested in what I am doing now and want to continue working on this page. I am also tired and want to stand up and stretch a bit. How close are those feelings to each other? Are they a yard or only an inch apart? Clearly the question is meaningless. If I ask how large each of these feelings is, how much room they take up, or even what their shape in space is, I shall again be asking meaningless questions. The principle of space does not apply in this realm. In distinction to the brain, consciousness is simply not located in space, and indeed is not located anywhere in the space-time-energy-matter universe in which all events in the sensory realm take place. This applies not only to consciousness, but also to all its observables. Our thoughts, our passions, our hopes and our memories cannot be related to each other by the same explanatory rules we use for dealing with wheels and pistons, exploding gasoline or moving cam shafts.

At a time when the study of consciousness was accepted as the central task of psychology and was being worked on by leading psychologists, this was clearly understood. Hugo Munsterberg put it thus in 1899:

> Primarily the inner experience has no spatial quality at all, and is thus neither in a room nor in a brain, space is a form of its objects, not of its own reality.[29]

Boris Sidis wrote in 1914:

> Psychic life is no doubt the concomitant of nervous brain activity, and certain psychic processes may depend on definite local brain processes, but the given psychic process . . . is not situated anywhere in space.[30]

In this absence of space as a meaningful concept in the Realm of Consciousness, we see one reason why there are no 'objects', no 'things' in this realm, only events. We define separate objects as objects separated by space. Without the existence of space there can be no separate objects, and therefore no objects are observed. Events, however, can be separated by time as well as by space, and time is a legitimate and valid guiding principle in the Realm of Consciousness.[31]

The concept of space is so important to the problems of para-psychology that I shall be discussing it in more detail later.

Just as there are aspects of the Realm of Sensory Experience, such as space, that do not exist in the Realm of Consciousness, the reverse is also true. In the Realm of Consciousness we find the observable 'purpose'. It does not exist in the sensory realm. Iron filings have no purpose in flying toward a magnet. If a card is placed before the magnet they will fly as far as its surface and remain pressed against it. They do not deflect around it or move at right angles to it until they can approach their goal directly.

But if you build a wall between Romeo and Juliet, the attraction between them does not keep them pressed on opposite sides of it. They will go around or over or under it, or Romeo will go back to the next town, buy a pickaxe and a stick of dynamite and come back and wreck the wall. They go through all of this clearly so that they can get as close to each other as nature will allow. Romeo and Juliet's purposes direct their actions.

In Romeo's consciousness there is the desire to get to Juliet; Juliet experiences a similar desire for Romeo. They both feel the pull of the perceived goal and strive for ways of achieving it. This is 'purpose', and it is a clear observable in this realm. To ignore it on the basis of a preconceived theory about reality is not permissible in science. In the Realm of Sensory Experience it would not be permissible to ignore 'matter' on the basis of a preconceived theory that all reality lies hidden behind a veil (in Eastern philosophy, the 'veil of Maya') and that therefore everything we see or touch is illusion. In the Realm of Consciousness, 'purpose' is a valid observable even though it does not exist in the sensory realm any more than the observable 'volume' exists in the domain of a flat, two-dimensional universe.

The observable 'purpose' is not a popular one in the social sciences. For historical reasons of which we are barely aware, we have tried, against all the evidence of our experience, to pretend it did not exist. So determined were we to make the necessary rejection of anthropomorphism in realms where it did not belong that in the great crusade we also threw it out of realms in which it *did* belong. Anthropomorphizing is legitimate and necessary in realms in which anthropos exists. In our attempts to drive *purpose* out of our conception of machines and billiard balls, we also tried to drive it out of our conception of consciousness.

Very little has been done in the field of parapsychology in exploring how purpose affects Type B perceptions. That so little has been done is a good indicator of the strength of the 'only-one-valid explanation' assumption. One exception to this is an important, but largely ignored, 1956 paper by the parapsychologist W. E. Cox. Cox pointed out that psi is usually analyzed in terms of the hypothetical 'route' by means of which the paranormal information arrives in the consciousness of the recipient. He suggested that analysis in terms of 'purpose' would be more valuable and offered the tentative preliminary classifications of 'Beneficial', 'Non-Beneficial', 'Trivial', and 'Detrimental'.[32]

It is so evident to all of us that 'purpose' is a major observable in the Realm of Consciousness (and in the Realm of Molar Behaviour) that it is difficult to see how its existence could be meaningfully questioned. And how should we question it without the purpose of doing so? In Alfred North Whitehead's words: 'Scientists who spend their life with the purpose of proving that it is purposeless constitute an interesting field of study.'[33]

In understanding the laws of each realm or domain we only need to relate the observables in that realm or domain. If I am dealing with thermodynamics, I deal with pressure, temperature, entropy, etc. I do not deal with observables from mechanics such as the position and momentum of individual particles.

Since purpose is an observable in the realm in which paranormal events take place, we have to consider it when trying to understand these events. This seems easy to comprehend. What is much harder to accept intellectually – and I shall deal with this in detail later – is that since space is *not* an observable in this realm, we do *not* have to consider it in our attempt to understand these events.

The last special aspect of the Realm of Consciousness we will examine here is the problem of what the term 'causation' means in this realm. In dealing with sensory reality, we consider an event to be explained 'as soon as we can show that it is necessarily connected with another fact that preceded it':[34] in other words, as soon as we have a law that states that given fact (or combination of facts) 'A', fact 'B' will follow. We establish these laws by repeating 'A' over and over and seeing that 'B' inevitably follows. Further, laws are frequently quantitative – different amounts of 'A' lead to different amounts of 'B'. In the sensory realm there is no problem here. We determine that 'A' causes 'B'. We predict that 'A' *will* cause 'B'.

Predictability is the way we test our laws and is generally seen as the hallmark of a scientific approach. The goal of science is seen as predictability.

It is true that we have had to make some variations in the realm of the very small. In this realm of subatomic particles, the realm of quantum mechanics, we have learned that we can never make the kind of exact predictions that we make in the sensory reality. If, in the realm of things we can see and touch, one billiard ball hits another, and we know the mass of each and the rate and direction of movement of the moving ball, we can predict with absolute assurance in which direction they will both move after the impact, how far they will travel and exactly where they will end up. This is what a good billiards player does with astounding accuracy. However, in the quantum mechanics realm, it is absolutely and *in principle* impossible to predict what specific event will happen next. To take an earlier example, if we have a mass of radium atoms and we know that they decay at a specific rate, it is impossible to predict *which* atom will decay next. It is not because we do not have enough knowledge that we cannot do this. It is simply impossible. 'Causation' in this realm is statistical, not specific. I can tell you precisely how large a percentage of the radium atoms will have decayed at any specific time, but not which ones. My statistical predictions can be very accurate; my specific ones cannot be more than guesses.

We have thus learned that in different realms the word 'causation' may mean different things. What does it mean in the Realm of Consciousness? How does it differ from the 'common-sense' definition of the sensory realm?

In the first place it differs in that we cannot establish any laws. As we have just seen, a law is established by repeating the same situation over and over and thus verifying that whenever we have 'A' then 'B' follows. However, as we have also seen, this is something we cannot do in consciousness. The same situation is *never* repeated. We cannot establish laws that will enable us to predict future events in consciousness because we cannot repeat the same situation and recreate 'A' to see if 'B' follows. We cannot predict what will happen, and thus cannot use predictability as a criterion for our having a science of consciousness or not having one. 'Causation' clearly differs in its meaning in this realm from the meaning it has in the sensory realm at least as much as it does in the quantum realm.

Since no situation repeats itself in consciousness, there is no true probability that a specific event (pattern of consciousness) will occur at any specific time until *after* it has occurred. Its probability is then 100 per cent. This is what we mean by saying that the past is determined, but the future is free. It is not a lack of knowledge that keeps us from knowing the exact probability of a future event in consciousness. There is no such probability.

In addition, laws in the sensory realm are usually quantitative; they involve numbering things so that arithmetical and algebraic procedures can be applied. A different amount of 'A' leads to a different amount of 'B' and these relationships can be stated in laws and equations. The Realm of Consciousness, however, is non-quantitative, and we cannot assign numbers to different amounts of the observables. This also means that we cannot accurately predict what is going to happen in consciousness as we can have no 'laws', in the sense of the word we usually apply, to guide us.

I am stressing the problem of predictability since 'causation' and 'predictability' are two sides of the same coin. If I can predict that a specific something is going to happen, this means that I know what caused it. If I know the cause of something, I can predict that it will happen or appear when the causes are present. Causation and predictability cannot be separated in any meaningful way. The importance of this for 'explaining' paranormal events will shortly become clear.

If we are dealing with a realm in which the observables cannot be quantified and in which no situation can be repeated, so that no laws can be established governing predictability, we cannot ever predict exactly when something will happen. (We are here discussing important events in consciousness such as falling in or out of love, experiencing strong emotions of joy, anger, or sadness; or major psi-events such as meaningful telepathic communications or death-bed apparitions.) *This is not a limitation on the knowledge we have, but a limitation on the knowledge we can have.* The nature of the realm forbids it.

If we cannot predict exactly when psi-events will happen, we cannot set up a technique that will make them happen on demand. This is precisely what parapsychologists have been trying to do, and felt that they *ought* to be able to do, for many years. They have accepted the statement of many of their critics that a repeatable experiment was the mark of a real science. A repeatable experiment in parapsychology is 'a psi-producing machine'. It means that 'psi-events will be produced and apparent if . . .'.[35] It implies accurate and exact predictability, 'a possibility in the Realm of Sensory Experience', but absolutely forbidden in the Realm of Consciousness by its Basic Limiting Principles. We can no more make a psi-producing machine than we can make a falling-in-love-producing machine, a creativity-producing machine, a machine that will tell us how an individual will be affected by a profound experience, such as the death of a loved one or a machine to produce deep and lasting religious feeling.

Certain things just cannot be done; certain devices cannot be made. Ever. These include a perpetual motion machine that does work in the sensory realm, a computer that will predict specific events in the microcosm (such as which radium atom will decay when) and a psi-producing machine. In each of these cases, the nature of the realm with which we are dealing forbids them.

We cannot exactly predict the future in the Realm of Consciousness because of the nature of the observables. This is a limitation by the very nature of things, not by the limitations of our present knowledge. It is as much a limitation as is, in the quantum realm, the Heisenberg limitation that we cannot know both the position and velocity of a particle at the same time. We are going to have to accept this in our psychological and parapsychological research. When Margaret Fuller, in one of her more bravura moments, exclaimed 'I accept the universe', Thomas Carlyle replied, 'Madame, you'd better.' We should do the same.

However, if we cannot predict the future in the Realm of Consciousness, there is something else that we can do. If, after an event has occurred, we look backward in time we can show the relationship of the events leading up to it. We can see how each conscious situation logically proceeded from the one before it and how the sequence logically and inexorably culminated in the event in which we are concerned. If we know enough about the total situation we can show how *each event that has already occurred* was determined and had to happen. But with no exact repetition possible, we can have no guides as to how to scientifically predict the future. In principle we cannot precisely predict what will happen next. Explanation in this realm means showing that past events had to happen as they did: future events are unpredictable. The past was determined; the future is free. The physicist Erwin

Schrödinger, describing this, quotes from Galsworthy's *The Dark Flower:*

> But that was it. . . . You never knew what was coming . . . and yet, when it came, it seemed as if nothing else could have come. That was queer – you could do anything you liked until you'd done it, but when you *had* done it, then you knew, of course, that you must always have had to. . . .[36]

A great playwright, say Shakespeare, writes a play. Analyzing it after he wrote it, we could, in theory, show how each character and line was inexorably determined by the interaction of Shakespeare's genetic inheritance and his experience. We could never, however, predict the exact lines of his next play. It is not from our lack of knowledge of his genetic background and his experience that we cannot predict these forthcoming lines. No matter how much we knew, we could not predict them any more than increased knowledge would enable us to know exactly which radium atom will decay next.

Try to conceive of a creative poet and what information you would need to predict exactly in advance his next poem. We might, on the basis of his past performance and present mood, make some general guesses – it would be a sonnet, pessimistic, about male-female relationships, and so on – but can we conceive of knowing enough to predict (that is, write in advance) the poem precisely as he will? It turns out that to know enough to predict the poem exactly, we would have to *be the poet:* to be identical with the poet in all aspects of genetic inheritance and experience. And be identical with him at the moment of writing – because he too will be surprised at how the poem turns out. Events in consciousness are private, singular, unpredictable.

Psychological phenomena defy all laws of the sensory realm. Nothing is quantifiable, no mechanical models can be made, there are no laws of conservation of energy, there is no such thing as spatial separation, and no such things as objects. The list could go on. *The great error of parapsychology has been to try to solve its problems as if they were physical problems from the sensory realm.*

In accepting the fact that there is a real difference between the Realm of Sensory Experience and the Realm of Consciousness, a difference of such profound magnitude that we cannot explain occurrences in one of them with the explanatory system of the other, we are flying in the face of long-held and deeply-felt beliefs. The philosopher M. Polanyi has pointed out:

> It is taken for granted among biologists that all manifestations of life can ultimately be explained by the laws governing inanimate matter. K. S. Lashley declared this at the Hixon symposium in 1948 as the common belief of all the participants without even consulting his distinguished colleagues. Yet this assumption is patent nonsense. The most striking feature of our own existence is our sentience. The laws of physics and chemistry include no conception of sentience, and any system wholly determined by these must be insentient. It may be to the interests of science to turn a blind eye on this central fact of the universe, but it is certainly not in the interest of truth.[37]

As Sir John Eccles has said, the Realm of Consciousness is unique in that there alone is the observable the recognition of the self.[38]

In one of his classic understatements, Sir Charles Sherrington wrote: 'Mind, meaning by that thoughts, memory, feelings, reasoning, and so forth, is difficult to bring into a class of physical things'.[39] It may be very hard to give up a long-held and unquestionably accepted idea such as that there is only one system of explanation for everything that is, but that is what we are going to have to do if we wish to make progress in parapsychology. The hardest part of advancement in human understanding is escaping from the old – getting past established doctrine. Once we can stop automatically accepting the old answers, the new ones can come into being.

'If you think we are waxworks, you ought to pay,' said Tweedledum to Alice. 'If you think we humans are machines, and our thoughts and feelings and actions can be interpreted on the same principles we use for machines, you have to pay,' we might well add in a statement directed to psychologists generally, and to parapsychologists in particular. The cost is not in a shilling ticket to the exhibition, but in any hope of ever making sense out of what it means to be a human being and out of human feeling, perception and behaviour: of ever making sense out of paranormal perceptions.

The idea that an entirely different kind of scientific model is needed in the human sciences from that needed in the basic physical sciences is not a new one. In the late nineteenth century and in the early part of this century a great deal of work was done to show how different these two necessary models are and how different are their methodologies, systems of data classification, validation procedures, prediction possibilities, and so forth. In Germany there was the extensive work of Willhem Windelband, a contemporary and friend of Freud, who carefully defined the differences between the *Naturwissenschaften,* the natural sciences, and the *Geisteswissenschaften,* the sciences of consciousness and behaviour. Ernest Rénan wrote of 'la science de l'humanité' and 'la science de la nature'. Long before them G. B. Vico (1668-1744) had demonstrated in detail that the science of history is very different in its basic methodology and types of results than those applicable to mathematics and the mechanical view of nature.

Gradually agreement developed on the differences between what was called 'nomothetic' science and 'ideographic' science. These terms, originated by Wilhelm Dilthey and developed further by Windelband, stressed the difference between 'generalizing knowledge' *(Erklären)* and 'individualizing knowledge' *(Verstehen).* The human sciences, the sciences of consciousness and behaviour, were of the second kind. Nomothetic science searches for, and is based on, general laws. Mathematics frequently plays an important role. Verification of ideas requires replication by experiment. Exact predictions are – at least in theory – made and tested.

Ideographic science seeks to understand the objects of its study as singular events, not as instances of universal laws. There are no exact predictions possible in principle, but after each event has occurred it is possible – in theory, at least – to look backward and see what led up to its occurrence; how it inexorably developed out of a previous total situation. Henri Bergson has demonstrated in some detail how this is the appropriate method for history.

The concept of prediction is quite different in these two approaches to science. In nomothetic science, to quote the physicist Erwin Schrödinger: 'What happens anywhere at a given moment depends only and unambiguously on what has been going on in the immediate neighbourhood "just a moment earlier". Classical physics rested entirely on this principle.'[40] It is plain from this definition that if we know enough about what is going on 'in the immediate neighbourhood', we can predict exactly what will happen next. Indeed, this is the test we use for the accuracy of our knowledge and the validity of our hypotheses.

In ideographic science, the problem of prediction is entirely different. Only after an event has occurred can we explain how it had to happen. No matter how much we knew about the local situation we could not predict what would happen next as each person at each moment is unique. Not only can we not predict how a person will behave on the basis of how other people have behaved in 'similar' situations (because our subject is unique and different from these other persons); we cannot even predict how *this* person will behave on the basis of his past reactions, because he is now different from how he ever was before. Further, since each situation is partially defined by how the individual perceives it, there are no 'similar' situations.

This may appear to be nitpicking and to be making a very great deal out of very small differences. Nevertheless, in the Realm of Consciousness and in the Realm of Meaningful Behaviour, these differences, while often small, are crucial enough to force us to change our entire model of science if we wish to obtain a better understanding of our data than we have so far managed to obtain in the social sciences generally and in parapsychology in particular. An apparently small difference may make a very great deal of difference, as Bertrand Russell once pointed out was the case with the notorious 'very small baby'.

To continue with our previous analogy: if we wish to know more about 'falling in love', we would apply ideographic methods, treat each case as an individual one, and − after it occurred − question and study the persons involved in detail (using not only traditional methods, but also new techniques for understanding the individual person). We would analyze what led up to the event, the personality structure and history of our particular Romeo and Juliet, and see, in retrospect, how these histories inexorably led up to the event. We would slowly build up our understanding of the processes involved, the kind of dynamic interaction that leads to and affects 'falling in love', but we would know that with this type of event we could never, *in principle,* make exact predictions about *who* would fall in love *when.* We could thus never design a repeatable experiment on the classical model.

We could, however, learn about those constellations of factors that made falling in love more or less likely. We could help an individual who had never fallen in love to remove those blocks within him that prevented it. (This is what a good psychotherapist does for a patient who suffers from the inability to love.) We would thus make it much more *likely* to happen, but could never predict precisely with whom and when the person we have helped would fall in love. We can predict that if a hundred persons are unable to fall in love and fifty come for psychotherapeutic help, then in our 'experimental group' (those working with a psychotherapist) there will be a higher percentage of individuals who will fall in love in the following five years than in the 'control' group (those who did not work with a therapist). We can test this prediction, we can even repeat the experiment many times and refine our hypothesis further, i.e., with the same *kind* of psychotherapist. But we can *never* predict precisely which persons will fall in love when.

We parapsychologists, however, feel that if we design our experiments *perfectly* we should be able to control and predict human behaviour precisely and in detail. Our main question is: How shall we make our designs and what group of factors shall we use? We no longer believe in some of the groupings that have been advanced in the past. The philosopher Hippolyte Taine said that if we knew enough about three factors – race, place, and time – we could explain and predict with absolute accuracy. This triad is no longer acceptable. Not only is the concept of race unpopular among scientists (particularly among those who wish to retain their academic posts), but the whole triad no longer 'feels' right to us.

However, we feel that there *is* somewhere a group of factors that – if (and when) we get them right – will do the job and make our experiments as precise as those we did in our beginner's course in college physics. For parapsychology perhaps something like MMPI Score (a personality test giving exact mathematical scores), Relationship Between Subject And Researcher, and Subject's State of Consciousness. That feels closer to the truth for us. We still hold onto Taine's basic idea that human behaviour is completely predictable, and so we should be able to build a psi-producing machine, a repeatable experiment of the kind found in nomothetic science.

Influenced by Windelband and this entire stream of philosophical research and development, Freud made it clear that the psychology of consciousness and the psychology of human behaviour fit the model of ideographic science and not the model of nomothetic science. Human behaviour, he demonstrated, could not be predicted in advance. Once it had happened, the methods of psychoanalysis could show why it and no other pattern of behaviour had occurred. The past could be explained as determined: the future could not be predicted; it was free.

In the interpretation of dreams, for example, the entities and actions of the dreams were examined and their meanings at different levels of consciousness explored until it was found how the history of the entity or action intersected with the history of the symptom being treated. The *properties* of the entity or action only had meaning in terms of this particular individual and in relation to the special and peculiar histories of the symptoms and dream segment for *this* person and his unique history. In Freud's words: 'Dream interpretation . . . without reference to the dreamer's associations . . . remains a piece of scientific virtuosity of the most doubtful value.'[41]

After the analysis of a dream, it is possible to show why this particular dream occurred at this time; but, in principle, it is impossible to predict exactly what the next dream will be. The most dedicated psychoanalyst, with his most fully analyzed and understood patient, would not 'dream' of essaying the task.

However, this insight, that different kinds of science needed different scientific models and methods, was lost to psychology in the great rush to ape the methods of the vastly and dramatically successful nineteenth-century physics and machine design. Since 1910, the major question of the social sciences has been – in Sigmund Koch's words – '*What* to emulate in the physical sciences?' Parapsychology really arrived at this point late, in the 1930s. What we parapsychologists failed to realize is that it is possible that social psychology is nomothetic (although this is far from proven), but that the psychology of consciousness and the psychology of individual behaviour are ideographic and therefore demand and need a different model of science, a different methodology, and have a different set of goals than the basic physical sciences; further, that it is in these last two realms that we observe psi phenomena – that we find Type B perceptions. As Jan Ehrenwald wrote: 'Psi phenomena have no independent existence of their own. They are observed only in the consciousness or behaviour of a human being.'[42]

As parapsychologists we have been trying our hardest to use nomothetic methods and models for the study of a field of knowledge that is adapted to ideographic methods, and feeling that we are failures for not succeeding. We have communicated this feeling of failure to our critics and reinforced them in their sense that this was the correct light in which to view us.

One of the central problems of designing a useful model and methodology for parapsychology is the question every science faces – how to *order* its data. The philosopher Jacob Bronowski has explored this matter in some detail and it may be useful to present four quotations from his *The Common Sense of Science*.[43]

> Order is the selection of one set of appearances rather than another because it gives us a better sense of the reality behind the appearances. (p. 48)

> Until science has passed through a long stage of observations and trial, it cannot develop a system of ordering its observations. (p. 46)

> A science which orders its thought too early is stifled. (p. 45)

> This question of order is the most difficult question in science. The notion of order cannot be defined on any ground except success. It cannot be put into a science in advance at all. It is not obviously silly to classify flowers by their colour; after all the bluer flowers do tend to be associated with colder climates and greater heights. There is nothing wrong with the system in advance. It simply does not work as conveniently and as instructively as Linaeus's classification by family likenesses. (p. 48)

It is easy to make an order of machine-made things such as new pennies or hairpins that are identical to our senses. We can find no difficulties and so can easily make classes of them. But in nature, we do not find this identical quality – all apples are different, as are all horses. The first generalizations we make, the first ordering of our observations of nature, is a vast jump of the human mind.

Typically, we make the first and subsequent orderings in two very different ways. We order some things on the basis of their properties – all apples are apples because they are round, red or green, juicy, come from a tree, and so forth. Other things we order on the basis of their history – this particular carving knife is to be avoided because I once cut myself with it; this particular flower attracts me because my mother grew them around our house when

I was a child. Much of the work of the philosopher Ernst Cassirer was devoted to the analysis of these two types of thought and he showed in detail how they both reflected in our language.

The history of thought, and of scientific thought in particular, has shown over and over again that many of our difficulties in solving our problems arise from the use of the wrong system of ordering our observations. The basic question is: Which method is appropriate to a given problem and set of observations?

It is now becoming increasingly clear that a science of psi must be a science of classes of entities made on the basis of their histories, not on the basis of their properties. Parapsychology, following the model of nineteenth-century physics, has tried to classify its observations of phenomena on the basis of their *properties.* This is how nomothetic science classifies things. However, ideographic science classifies them on another basis – their *history.* Our observations of the way psi phenomena occur are all in this direction, but because we thought it was *scientific* we have held to the properties model. We have remained steadfast and loyal to the inapplicable ordering system we chose too early in our development. And we all know better. For example, I might ask a group of experienced parapsychologists which of the two following examples of crisis telepathy are more likely to happen.

1. X has once had a love affair with Y that is of deep meaning to both of them. She is in a fatal automobile accident 3000 miles away and he has a death-bed apparition of her at that time.

2. X is tall, red haired, a lawyer, and has a limp in his left leg. Y also is over 6 feet tall, red haired, a lawyer, and has a limp in the left leg. Further, both of them have one blue and one grey eye. They have never met or heard of each other. Y is killed in an automobile accident and X has a death-bed apparition of him at the same time.

As anyone with experience in this field will tell you, No. 1 is the kind of event widely reported, No. 2 is not. Yet in the second case the participants in the psi occurrence had many more properties in common with each other. The psi event does not occur because they have no *history* in common.

One of the clearest signposts in this direction that we have had is the famous Fisk-West experiment.[44] Identical packs of cards – in all their known properties – were sent to a group of widely scattered participants who attempted to guess their order without opening them. Some of the cards were shuffled by Fisk, some by West. The card guessers had no means of knowing who had shuffled each pack, nor that there were different shufflers. Packs shuffled by Fisk were guessed at a much higher success rate (a statistically significantly higher rate) than were the cards shuffled by West. The cards were alike in their properties, different in their histories.

> Neither the physical properties of the ESP target nor its positioning relative to the subject seemed to have any effect on the subject's scores. Neither distance nor intervening material barriers were relevant variables in the psi experiment.[45]

In the 1970s, Charles Honorton, one of our best and most experienced parapsychologists, made a great and sustained effort to devise an ideal set of 1056 targets for experimental work. He showed great ingenuity in varying the properties of these targets so that it would be possible to judge the accuracy of a 'hit' with great precision. Nothing much came from the work with the completed set; the basic assumption that variation on the basis of properties would be useful simply did not bear fruit.

The idea that targets in psi-research must be chosen on the basis of their histories, not their properties, is related to the fact that the 'homoeostatic' forces in the Realm of Consciousness are primarily oriented to maintaining the stability of relationships, not to the stability of entities or their properties. Cassirer has put it that the 'constancies', the crucial relating factors, required for an understanding of cultural and individual behaviour is 'not that of properties, but of meanings'.[46]

When we have tried to vary the properties of the target in parapsychological experiments we have had no success in getting different rates of target hitting. We could make the target large or small, in a known or unknown language, of different colours, make the task more or less complex – the success rate remains about the same. It doesn't seem to matter at all whether the psi task is complex or simple, inside or outside of a Faraday cage, as close as the next room or halfway across the planet; the properties of it do not affect the success rate. In direct and in proxy sittings by mediums, the results are more or less the same. The evidence that we must give up this classification system for our experimental design and our theorizing is clear. Yet still we have ignored it. A good medium will frequently ask for an object whose history is related to the person or subject under investigation. Many of them have preferred to work psychometrically – whether awake or in trance – since we started investigating serious mediums. None of them, to my knowledge, ever seemed to care much about the size, colour, hardness, or chemical make-up of the object to be psycho-metrized. They cared only about its history. However, since they were only serious mediums who often had Type B perceptions, and not successful scientists who designed *machines that ran,* we ignored their clear preferences and what we might have learned from them.

Overall we have attained – with the ordering system we have been using – roughly the kind of consistency of results that might be obtained by classifying flowers by their colour. 'This,' writes Bronowski, 'is the important step in every science: the construction of a first order which is reasonable in itself and which holds to the experimental facts that are known.'[47]

This is a step that we have not taken. We have chosen an ordering system that is 'reasonable in itself', but not one that held to the known facts. This is certainly one reason why our results have been inconsistent and sporadic.

It is interesting that, as Bronowski has demonstrated,[48] the history of science shows that until a science has found a valid system of ordering its data, it has no social standing – it is not recognized as a valid science nor its practitioners as scientists. As we parapsychologists bewail our outcast position in the community of science, we might ponder a possible causal connection here.

Let us now sum up and see what we have found out about the Realm of Consciousness, the realm in which paranormal occurrences are observed. We have looked at ten aspects of this realm.

1. There are no 'things', only processes.

2. There is only private access to the data. Only one person can make the observations.

3. The observables are non-quantitative in principle.

4. Relationships tend to be constant, not properties.

6. Purpose *is* an observable.

7. Situations never repeat themselves; therefore there can be no exact prediction of situations.

8. Any aspect of consciousness that is examined is changed by the examination.

9. The relevant scientific method is that of ideographic science, not that of nomothetic science.

10. The relationship between the persons, or persons and 'things' in a Type B perception is determined by their *histories,* not by their *properties.*[49]

It is in a metaphysical system, a way of explaining how-things-work, that includes these ten factors that we shall have to look for our understanding of the paranormal. In the following chapters, I shall show that within this system they can be understood with no more difficulty than anything else that occurs in the Realm of Consciousness.[50]

5

WHAT IS CONSCIOUSNESS AND WHERE IS IT?

In order to begin to explore the questions of the chapter from the viewpoint of modern *realm* theory, let us start with a simpler problem. Where does 'volume' come from? We all know what the word 'volume' means. It is the size, measure or amount of anything in three dimensions. A pint bottle is a container with height, width and length. It holds a volume of one pint. A lake holds a larger volume. If we want to find the volume of a box with inside dimensions two inches long, three inches wide and four inches high, we multiply two times three times four, and say that the box has a volume of 24 cubic inches. A structure must have three dimensions – height, width and length – to have volume.

A two-dimensional structure does not have volume. I draw a square on a sheet of paper and say, 'What is the volume of the square?' The question is meaningless. I might as well ask how loud is a length of three metres or what is the colour of the square root of minus one. There is no such thing as volume in a two-dimensional universe – such as that in which the drawn square exists. Then where did volume come from when we add the extra dimension of height?

When we go from the domain of a two-dimensional universe to the adjacent domain of a three-dimensional universe, a new observable, volume, 'appears'. It is suddenly and absolutely there. Science finds no particular interest in asking where it came from. We have little curiosity about this question. What we *do* ask in science is, 'How shall we study it?' 'How shall we learn to understand the new observable?' 'What can we say about it?' And for these questions, science has a method.

The method consists of asking, 'What are its relationships to the other observables we find in this domain?' In the domain of a three-dimensional universe we find the observables of distance, direction, angle, height, length, width, area, volume, and shape of figure. We study volume by examining its relationships to the other observables in the three-dimensional domain. We may also study the relationships of these observables to the observables of adjacent domains such as a two-dimensional universe. We do not worry very much over the question, 'What *is* the two-dimensional universe?' It is the domain, the artificial slice of reality in which we perceive only two dimensions. We constrict ourselves to perceiving and dealing with reality as if this is, for the moment, the way it is constructed. Using this focused and limited perception we then say: 'What do we observe?' We perceive certain things – such as length, breadth, direction, angle – and ask what the relationships between these observables are. In this way we construct a science, but we name it – in this case, 'plane geometry'. In this science we deal with the observables in their own terms and follow our study of their relationships wherever it leads. We try to be aware of our assumptions, both the limited ones of the particular field (e.g., that we are dealing with a flat surface, not a curved one) and our general ones (such as that all observables in a domain are related lawfully to each other). We find other domains that are related to this in such a way that we can measure the relationships of some of the observables we find in them to the observables we find in the domain we are studying.

Groups of domains require the same metaphysical system to make their data coherent. They use the same definitions of the 'guiding principles' such as 'space', 'time', 'causality'. These groups each make up a 'realm'. A domain that needs a different model of reality, a different metaphysical system, in order to make sense out of the data we find in it belongs in a different realm. In short, all domains in a realm use the same model of reality.

Thus, we do not need to worry very much over the question, 'What is the universe of consciousness?' It is the realm, the artificial slice of reality, in which we perceive only our inner, non-physical activity. We constrict ourselves to perceiving and dealing with reality as if this is, for the moment, the way it is constructed. Using this focused and limited approach, we then say, 'What do we observe?' We perceive certain things – such as process, intensity, sense of identity, clarity, mood, presence or absence of specific information – and ask what relationships between these observables are.

Indeed, the definition of this realm passes no particular problem. We all solve it easily. As James pointed out so clearly:

> All people unhesitatingly believe that they feel themselves thinking, and that they distinguish the mental state as any inward activity or passion, from all the objects with which it may cognitively deal.[1]

'The boundary-line of the mental,' wrote James, 'is certainly vague. It is better not to be too pedantic, but to let the science be as vague as the subject, and to include such phenomena as feelings, desires, cognitions, reasonings, decisions and the like, if by doing so we can throw any light on the main business at hand.'[2]

We must emphasize that science today does not ask what something *is*, but rather how it relates to other observables in the same, and perhaps adjacent, domains. Even the formal definition of volume – length times height times width expressed in cubic units – is a statement of relationship, not of what *is*.

We have learned that 'What is' questions lead around in a circle and do not get us very far. When Clerk-Maxwell, one of the greatest intellects in the history of physics, applied the 'What is' question to the terms 'matter' and 'energy' he ended up with:

> We are acquainted with matter only as that which may have energy communicated to it from other matter and which may, in its turn, communicate energy to other matter.
>
> Energy, on the other hand, we know only as that which, in all natural phenomena, is continually passing from one portion of matter to another.[3]

In a similar vein, if we wish to ask the 'What is' question about other entities, we tend to come up with definitions such as:

> An electron is a region of space with mass, charge and velocity that attracts protons and repels other electrons.
>
> A proton is a region of space with mass, charge and velocity that attracts electrons and repels other protons.

Science does not ask what entities are. We ask rather how they vary in relation to the degree of presence of other variables in this domain. This extremely important, but often forgotten, methodological point in science is illustrated by the old story of the professor who asked the student, 'What is electricity?' The student replied, 'I have forgotten.' The professor then exclaimed, 'Oh my God! The only man in the world who knew, and he has forgotten!'

If science does not ask, 'What is volume, what is energy, or what is matter?' why have we been constantly asking, 'What is consciousness?' and 'What is psi?' The reason is, of course, that these are so dramatic, so startling, when we stop to think about them, that we feel that they are somehow 'other', somehow diferent, and that they demand an explanation. They certainly do feel this way, but this does not mean that we must abandon the methods so long and laboriously worked out by science in our search for understanding.

Instead of continuing to ask the questions of medieval science such as 'What is mind?' 'What is consciousness?' 'What is psi?' we must, if we wish the methods of modern science to aid us in our search for understanding, ask the questions that twentieth-century science finds it legitimate and helpful to ask. These are, for example, the questions of how the presence or absence of identifiable paranormal occurrences varies with the degree of presence of the other entities and observables found in the same domain in which we observe the occurrences. This, of course, has been done by many of the students and researchers in the field, but has not, to my knowledge, ever been formally presented to find out where a clear statement of this approach would lead. In Chapter 10 I shall show how this sort of definition of the way modern science works can lead to a design for a research programme on the paranormal events that have been most neglected by modern parapsychology – such as death–bed apparitions – because it was not thought possible to be 'scientific' when studying them.

We are forced to the conclusion that the question, 'What is consciousness?' is not one in which modern science is either interested or equipped to answer. Perhaps, however, we can find an answer to the question, '*Where* is consciousness?' Indeed, this is a question to which we all intuitively believe we have the answer. 'It is located a couple of inches behind my eyes.' Here is 'where I feel myself to be'.[4]

On this point science seems to back us up. We believe that the fields of human biology and physiology have come to the conclusion that my consciousness is located in my brain. It is within my skull. When I assume this, however, *I am assuming that consciousness exists in space and that, furthermore, it exists in the same kind of space as my skull.*

One of the least understood (and certainly least emotionally accepted) implications of the Planck-Einstein revolution in science is that concepts such as space, time, causality, and observation may have different meanings in diferent realms of experience. The meaning appropriate for a particular realm is the *only meaning of the term that is acceptable for experiment and theory in that realm.* No one meaning has priority except in the realm in which it belongs.

We are, however, so committed to the usual 'common-sense' view of space and time that one of the major and crucial tests of a person's sanity is whether they can specify their position in space and time, and whether their specifications agree with those of the examiner.

In the *macrocosm,* the realm of experience in which things are too large or moving too rapidly in respect to the observer to be – even theoretically – seen or touched, the term 'space' takes on a completely different meaning than it does in the realm accessible to the senses. It loses its independent existence. It merges with the concept of time, and only the new concept 'space-time' is valid for this realm. As generations of teachers of theoretical physics have tried to teach their students, *only* this concept of 'space' applies in this realm and any use of concepts from other realms – such as the space we use in our everyday comings and goings, the space that we use to tie our shoelaces in or through which we travel to London – will only lead us into confusions, into struggling hopelessly with imaginary problems, and into facing apparently impossible and startling data.

In the realm of the *mesocosm,* the realm of experience accessible to our senses, the 'middle range', space is what we ordinarily conceive it to be. It is the 'empty' space of Newton, filled in part by objects. It is the space of Euclidean geometry.

The concept of space in the *microcosm,* the realm of experience in which things are too small to be – even theoretically – seen or touched, is still unclear. We know only that it is different from space in the realm of experience accessible to the senses. Physics is still struggling with the problem of how to define space in this realm so that the data will make most sense. The present discussions in physics of the EPR paradox and Bell's theorem are aspects of the present search for a definition of space in the microcosm.

The physicist Pascual Jordan has pointed out the importance of this for parapsychology. He states that we must change our conception of space in our work:

> We must adopt a radically different attitude, remembering that three-dimensional space, as we usually conceive it, is not an immediate experience, but the result of prior work by our mind and prior condition of what we may observe.[5]

Emotionally, however, we believe that there is only one 'real' space. This is the space of vision and touch, the space necessary for our everyday biological survival as we cross busy highways and shop for food in the supermarket. So overwhelming is the input from our eyes and skin (forming more than two-thirds of the nerve fibres running to our central nervous system), so strong are the historical forces telling us that this is a world where only what you can see or touch is *really* real, that we find it hard to take these other concepts of space seriously. We find it hard to believe that they are more than inventions that define space for some minor special purposes, but are no more 'really' real than the broomstick of the Wicked Witch of the North.

If, however, there is one lesson to be learned from the progress of science in some areas (and the lack of progress in others) in the past eighty years, it is that there is a new commandment: 'Thou shalt not take concepts from one realm of experience and use them in another.'[6]

Physical entities accessible to the senses exist in sensory-realm space, and when they are separate in this space they are separate entities. Sensory-realm space has certain geometric qualities. Consciousness, however, does not exist in physical space. It has no material qualities. The space that consciousness exists in has completely different qualities from physical space.

When we speak or think of the mind as 'in' the brain (or even 'in' the body) we are doing violence to our observations. We are saying that consciousness has a spatial location, that it has size, material form, shape, boundaries. These are not aspects of the observables of consciousness. To speak of the number of square or cubic feet that your consciousness takes up is as nonsensical as speaking of the smell of the number 174, or the voltage of the concept of group process. One cannot, at will, add entities to a realm, or attributes of the entities we find there, without landing in a semantic disaster.

> No one has the right to attribute positions, sizes, shapes or colours to things which, by their very nature, cannot bear such qualities. One might as well assign smell to a light beam.[7]

In the Realm of Consciousness, the term 'space' has an entirely different meaning than it has in the Realm of Sensory Experience. In the Realm of Consciousness, if we carefully examine what we observe there, we find that there is no geometric space. Geometry exists in the space we observe in outside and material objects – in the realm accessible to the senses. It does not apply to events, to observables, in consciousness. Geometric space, with its ability to be quantified, the space in which we can use terms like yards or miles or circular or 90^0 angle, is simply not applicable to the Realm of Consciousness. Our observables in it do not have length or breadth or height. An idea and an emotion cannot legitimately be described as an inch apart or at right angles to each other. Your consciousness cannot legitimately be described as being two feet north of mine. The geometric space of the sensory realm does not apply to consciousness any more than does the space-time of the macrocosm or the personal space of the realm of meaningful behaviour.

Much of the problematic nature of parapsychology comes from the assumption that consciousness can be located and bounded in space and that, *since it can be so located and bounded,* it cannot communicate with other consciousnesses located in different portions of space without some sort of communication system. We have confused different realms. The observables in the sensory realm are located in geometric space. The observables of consciousness are not. In Wilder Penfield's words, 'one cannot assign the mind a position in space'.[8]

I do not ask how the temperature of one sub-atomic particle (one *on*) is communicated to another. The observables would be completely confused if I did. Similarly, the problem of how one consciousness communicates with another across space is a confusion of realms. I do ask how temperature varies with variations of different observables, both those of the domain of mechanics and those in thermodynamics. If I wish to study psi occurrences, I will ask how they vary with different observables and combinations of observables in the domain of consciousness and with the domains of meaningful behaviour, brain states, etc. These are the legitimate questions of science.

We are facing here the problem that parapsychology has considered to be fundamental: How does the information get across the space from one consciousness to another? This is the problem that parapsychologists have struggled and struggled with in vain. Since it did not seem possible of solution, many of the critics of the field have concluded that the information did *not* cross the distance and that therefore there was no such thing as a psi occurrence. How shall we solve this conundrum? What answer can we find to this problem?

The answer is surprisingly simple from the viewpoint of modern science, from the viewpoint of realm theory. There *is* no problem. It is a false conundrum built on a fundamental semantic and conceptual error.

It is simply not legitimate to say that because the *bodies* of two subjects in an experiment are 300 miles apart, that their *consciousnesses* are also 300 miles apart. In the geometric space that their bodies exist in, the 300 miles makes a difference. Their consciousnesses do not exist in geometric space; the term 300 miles makes as little sense in the realm of consciousness, the realm in which their thoughts and feelings exist, as to say that they are 300 foot pounds or 300 volts apart.

'If we are not talking about material objects, it is futile and misleading to talk about spatial separations,' wrote Whately Carrington.[9] Our old habits make this hard to conceive. It seems obvious to us that consciousness has spatial location, and that the problem of the communication of separate minds is therefore a real problem. Modern science has no doubt, however, that it is meaningless to speak of space without matter, or gravitation without matter, or matter without space, or either of them without time; or to speak of a triangle with only two sides. Similarly, the size and shape *and location in space* of consciousness is as meaningless a subject as if we were speaking of the latitude and longitude of the Law of Diminishing Returns, or of the shape and texture of an electron.

This concept, that non-material entities cannot be located in three-dimensional space *and cannot be bounded in that space,* is little

understood in the history of psychical research and in parapsychology. (Morris Raphael Cohen wrote in this context: 'I
should refer to spiritists who locate disembodied spirits in space as
cryptomaterialists.')[10]

It is not only 'spirits' who cannot be located in space. (One is
reminded of the famous remark of the mystic Jacob Boehme, when
asked where the soul went at the death of the body. Boehme
answered: 'There is no necessity for it to go anywhere.')
Consciousness also cannot be located in space. In the Realm of
Consciousness, the term 'space' does not apply. And, if this is so,
then the central problem of parapsychology changes considerably.
We are no longer dealing primarily with the problem of how
information gets from one consciousness to another across an
intervening space.

An ESP event, a psi occurrence, starts out as an observable in
consciousness. It starts as something we know or we feel. (Perhaps
the work of Ian Stevenson has made this most clear.[11]) If we wish to
understand more about psi, if we wish to make progress in a
scientific sense, we must deal with it as an observable in the Realm
of Consciousness. We must use in our search the concepts that
apply in this realm, not those that apply in some other.

How do things get from one place to another? Things or information, the situation is the same. It is *only* a problem in realms in
which there is a 'where', a 'place' in which things can be located and
their boundaries defined. In realms in which this is not true, the
problem does not exist.

We have been fooled because we have such a strong impression
that our consciousness is located within our body. This seems to
lead to the problem of how the information gets from one body to
another.

This is far from a new point in the history of our field and in the
history of science itself. In 1925, to take only one example, R.
Tischner stated it clearly:

> Psychics is one of the fields in which the natural scientist likes to
> apply his theories with a naive consequentiality; he assumes,
> without any epistemological or psychological qualms that the
> psychical – which does not exist in space – will follow the
> mechanical laws of space, and builds airy hypothetical structures
> for that purpose.[12]

G. N. M. Tyrrell wrote in 1953: 'I . . . refuse to admit that the conscious self of a person who is talking to me in the same room is present in that room, or, indeed, is anywhere in space.'[13]

William James repeatedly pointed out that consciousness did not exist in the 'common-sense' space of the sensory realm, and that it was not material in the usual sense of the word. In a typical paragraph on this subject he wrote:

> It is not as if there were a bounded room where the minds in possession had to move up or make place and crowd together to accommodate new occupants. Each new mind brings its own edition of the universe of space along with it, its own room to inhabit; and these spaces never crowd each other – the space of my imagination, for example, in no way interferes with yours. The amount of possible consciousness seems to be governed by no law analogous to that of the so-called conservation of energy in the material world. When one man wakes up, or one is born, another does not have to go to sleep or die, in order to keep the consciousness of the universe at a constant quantity.[14]

This understanding, however, that consciousness must be comprehended in the realm in which it is observed, has been largely ignored in both psychology and parapsychology.

It is hard for us to realize that visual perspective is a convention, a fifteenth-century invention for the purpose of making distance look real on a two-dimensional surface. If we think that this is 'real', then how much harder is it for us to realize that the concept of empty, geometric space itself is a convention, a useful and necessary invention if we are to deal with some realms of experience, a useless and semantically disastrous one when we deal with others.

In Western thought, space separates objects. It is interesting to speculate how different parapsychology would be today if, in the West, we had the Japanese viewpoint that the space between objects has definite shape and *connects* the objects. The space between, the 'interval', is called the *ma*. It is perceived in Japan as being as real as the objects it connects.

Once it is plain that psi occurrences – Type B perceptions – are events in consciousness and not events 'out there' in the sensory world, much of its mysterious and peculiar quality – its 'spookiness' – disappears. We leave these attributes behind, with the concepts of geometric space and clock time that brought them into being. No longer must telepathy somehow get across the yards or miles between one subject and another, nor span the hours or days separating the observer from the event. In the space and time of consciousness, as well as in the personal space and personal time within which meaningful human perceptions and actions take place, feelings and attitudes determine how far entities and events are apart in space and time. They also determine when they are not apart at all.

The attributes that appear to exist in the 'outside' objects we perceive are, in large part at least, determined by the sense through which we perceive them. If I perceive a piano by sight, it has the attributes of shape, colour and so forth; if I perceive it by touch, of hardness, smoothness, and shape; if by hearing, of pitch, volume, and so on; if by smell, perhaps the odour of varnish. Sight and touch also give it the attribute of location in space, and this tends to be reinforced by the perception through the other senses. These attributes are perceived as 'real', and indeed *are* real in the realm of experience we are dealing with – the Realm of Experience of Things Accessible to the Senses. It is this realm that consciousness generally deals with and into which it disappears as 'a glass and a transparency'. It requires a hard and consistent effort of will, 'art and pains', as Locke said, to deal with any other realm in its own terms.

Crucial to our exploration is the fact that the attributes consciousness perceives in the 'outside' world are very different from the attributes of consciousness itself. When we focus our attention on our own inner experience, when we begin to examine the attributes of the realm of consciousness, we find not a single one of the attributes we have described above as found in our piano. We find no browns, blacks or white, no right angles or plane surfaces, no pitch or volume. Nor do we find a location in space delimited by boundaries. Attributes perceived in the outside world are very different from the attributes of consciousness.

One of the attributes that is found in the Realm of Experience Accessible to the Senses, but is not found in the Realm of Consciousness, is that of location in space delimited by boundaries. Although we tend to feel that our consciousness is located in our heads, this is a result of cultural conditioning, rather than of objective exploration of the entities and attributes of the Realm of Consciousness. It was not until Alcmaeon studied the relationship of brain injury and consciousness in the sixth century BC that the relationship of consciousness to the brain was known by Western society, and there are still a good many 'primitive' cultures that locate consciousness in other areas of the body, if they locate it anywhere at all.

There is certainly a strong feeling on our parts that our consciousness is *in* our brain and therefore in the room and in the same kind of space as are ordinary sensory objects. The strongest 'proof' that is generally given of this is that if one damages the brain, the mind is not present any longer.

This, of course, is a far weaker argument than it sounds at first hearing. For example, the situation could be analogous to my seeing Walter Cronkite on my television set. As long as my set is in good condition he is present to me. If my set malfunctions in certain ways, his delivery is so distorted and garbled that he makes no sense at all. Damage the set further and he is no longer present to me, but his existence in the studio is in no way compromised.

It is of further interest that many leading specialists in brain function, such as Sir Charles Sherrington and Wilder Penfield, have come to the conclusion that brain must be regarded as an organ of 'liaison' with the mind and not as consciousness itself or as an organ that generates consciousness. Penfield states categorically that brain and consciousness are two entirely different things and that all the modern evidence from brain research supports this view.[15]

Even if I am convinced that my consciousness is located in my brain, and 'feel' its presence somewhere behind my eyes and between my ears (not as a good Trobriand Islander would – in my liver), I peer inward in vain for its boundaries. Where does it stop? Is it a ball shape with a diameter of two inches? Is it limited by the surface of the cortex? By the meninges? By the skull? The questions bring no answers. I know where the outside of a vase is, and where the outside of my skin is, but not where the outside of my consciousness is. It is not, to my most careful perception, limited in space.

There are clearly relationships between my body, my brain and my consciousness. I cannot feel a pain in your leg. I can feel it in mine. But the relationships are those of observables in one domain to observables in another, not relationships between observables in the same domain. The observable 'temperature' is not in the domain of mechanics, it is in the domain of thermodynamics. Temperature is not an aspect of a particle (as is mass or velocity); it is related to and dependent on the attributes of large numbers of particles, but is in a different domain. If I try to deal with temperature as an aspect of a particle, I am in real trouble. I am in a semantic mess that it is difficult to escape from. The same is true if I consider location to be an aspect of consciousness.

I have discussed in earlier chapters the fact that space is different in different realms of experience. In the Realm of Consciousness the term is meaningless. Perceptions of different parts of the process of consciousness do not reveal that some are spatially further away from others and that others are spatially nearer. The terms simply do not apply any more than the term 'temperature' applies to an electron, or indeed to anything in the Realm of the Too-small-to-see-or-touch.

And herein lies one application of the insight of 'intentional inexistence' to parapsychology. If I ask how the temperature of one molecule affects the temperature of another I am involved in a false problem. I have mixed up entities and attributes of one realm of experience with the entities and attributes of another. No matter how ingenious I am in dealing with the question, no matter how many precise and careful experiments I devise and carry out, I shall fail to answer the question.[16]

We have worked very hard to arrive at some sort of an answer as to how Type B experiences could happen – how the information could get from one consciousness to another. In spite of our attempts, in spite of the fact that we have had men and women of very high ability, training and dedication spend great time and energy on the problem, we have not the ghost of an idea of how to find a solution. It is part of the faith of science that if serious people work for a long time on a question and cannot find an answer, then they are asking the wrong question. The question of how information is transmitted across a space between two consciousnesses has been the central question of parapsychology, the focus around which we have designed many of our experiments and towards which we have directed much of our speculation. From the viewpoint of modern science it is a false question. It assumes the presence of space between consciousnesses. It assumes that consciousness is bounded and delimited in space. Neither of these assumptions are valid.

Let us be clear about this. The brain is in the Realm of Experience of Things Accessible to the Senses. The brain exists in space and is bounded in space. How information travels from one brain (or one computer) to another is a legitimate question. The brain and consciousness, however, are in different realms of experience and questions valid in one realm are not necessarily valid in another. To return to our analogy, a molecule is related to a sizeable mass – say of iron. We can legitimately ask the temperature of the mass of iron. The mass of iron is made up of molecules. We cannot, however, legitimately ask the temperature of the molecules. They are in different realms of experience. To ask the temperature of the individual molecules, or how the temperature of one is transmitted to another, is meaningless. It is legitimate to ask how information travels from one brain to another, not, however, to ask how it travels from one consciousness to another.

Hardness, colour and malleability are characteristics of the mass of iron and – although they depend on molecular structure – must be dealt with as part of the Realm of Experience Accessible to the Senses. We cannot meaningfully ask 'how hard', 'what colour', or 'how malleable' a molecule is. These terms belong in a different realm of experience than the molecules. Paranormal events (Type B perceptions) are events in consciousness – although certainly related to brain structure and physiology – and must be dealt with as events in the Realm of Consciousness, not as events in the Realm of Experience Accessible to the Senses.[17] And in the Realm of Consciousness spatial location and spatial distance do not exist.

We are dealing here with a subtle, but very important point. Questions that may legitimately be asked, and statements that may be made, when an entity is considered from the viewpoint of one realm of experience have no meaning when the entity is considered from the viewpoint of another. It is legitimate to ask if a block of steel is harder than a block of lead. It is not legitimate or meaningful to ask if the atoms of which they are composed are harder in the steel block than they are in the lead one. It is legitimate to say that the block of steel may be either stationary or in motion. It is not legitimate to say that the electrons in the atoms of the block may be either stationary or in motion. Similarly, it is legitimate to say that the brain of an individual is located at such and such a place and bounded in such and such a way. It is not legitimate to say that his mind is located at such and such a place or bounded in such and such a way.

Parapsychology has been operating under the assumption that consciousness is *in* the brain, and that therefore the problem of distance is a real one. There is certainly no question today of the relationship of brain and mind. Four ounces of alcohol will affect the brain and then the mind. Psychological stimuli can affect the brain and alter its chemistry to a marked degree. Nevertheless, the two kinds of effect, resembling each other – to use Eddington's example again – as much as a telephone number resembles a subscriber, are not the same. They cannot be validly dealt with in the same way or explained in the same metaphysical system. They are not only in different domains of experience; they are in different realms of experience.

6

PARAPSYCHOLOGY
AND THE REALM OF
MEANINGFUL BEHAVIOUR

*The general failure to grasp the significance of the many elements that
contribute to man's sense of space may be due to two mistaken notions: (1)
that for every effect there is a single and identifiable cause; and (2) that a
man's boundary begins and ends with his skin. If we can rid ourselves of
the need for a single explanation, and if we can think of man as
surrounded by a series of expanding and contracting fields which provide
information of many kinds, we shall begin to see him in an entirely
different light.*[1]

We have been concerned in the previous chapter with space in the
Realm of Consciousness. This is one realm where psi phenomena
are observed and in which its problems of psi must be resolved. As I
have pointed out, space in the microcosm, space in the sensory
realm, space in the macrocosm, and space in consciousness are all
different from each other. There is also another realm, of particular
interest to parapsychologists, in which the term 'space' again has a
completely different meaning. This is the Realm of Meaningful
Behaviour. In this realm, we observe an individual's *response* to a psi
occurrence — a Type B perception. He acts on it — becoming sad,
distressed or initiating inquiries after a death-bed apparition. He
may tell others about it, or send a letter to the Society for Psychical
Research. He engages in *molar* behaviour, related to the psi
occurrence. The realm of experience dealing with such activity is
the Realm of Meaningful Behaviour. Here we go to the store,
prepare a meal, flirt with a neighbour, the hound pursues, the hare

flees. In this realm belong many of those 'anecdotal' psi occurrences that first sparked our interest in the field. Here space is 'personal space', and any valid comprehension of meaningful (molar) behaviour must use this definition of space.

I do not plan to explore personal space in detail here. It has been done very well elsewhere, such as in the work of the anthropologist E. T. Hall. An entire scientific field calling itself 'proxemics' is now devoted to its analysis. A few comments, however, are in order.

Molar behaviour is accomplished in a space within a space. The individual perceptually surrounds himself with a bubble of personal space. This moves, with him as the centre, through the perceived geometric space of sensory reality. This bubble is quite complex, composed, according to Hall, of at least four separate layers: 'intimate space', 'individual space', 'social space', and 'public space'. Behaviour towards other persons in each of these spaces is quite different. The thickness and *meaning* of the layers vary with different cultural groups, and Hall has shown quite convincingly that much of the misunderstandings between different cultural groups can often be traced to these differences.

In personal space, *distances* are divided into three classes: 'too close', 'correct', and 'too far' for the particular type of interaction the individual wants with others. Directions are in three planes: 'Above-below', 'before-behind', and 'left-right'. It is obvious that these coordinates are very different from those of the geometric space within which the bubble of personal space moves.[2]

One obvious difference, for example, is that in geometric space all location points have the same value, all are equal; none are in any way more significant than the others. In personal space there is one point (the centre where the planes meet) that is of very different value from *all* the rest of space, from every other point. This centre, where the 'I' is perceived to be located and from which or toward which all action flows, is unique and not equal to any other point: 'Euclidean space is characterized by the three basic attributes of continuity, infinity, and uniformity.'[3] Personal space does not have any of these three attributes.

Further, we behave differently to persons in each 'surround' of personal space. We talk 'at' those in public space; 'to' those in our individual space. We discuss things with a small group of friends in social space. A close friend is talked to in individual space; if the friend comes closer, into our intimate space, our response changes.

Another individual is allowed into our intimate space only for amative or combative purposes.

A quotation from the linguist Martin Joos seems both relevant and suggestive to our present exploration:

> An intimate utterance [an utterance made to someone in our intimate space] pointedly avoids giving the addressee information from outside of the speaker's skin. The point ... is simply to remind (hardly 'inform') the addressee of some feeling inside the speaker's skin.[4]

A description of the boundary of intimate and of individual space that will be recognizable as being valid to all of us was written by the poet W. H. Auden:

> Some thirty inches from my nose
> The frontier of my person goes,
> And all the untilled air between
> Is private *pagus* or demesne.
> Stranger, unless with bedroom eyes
> I beckon you to fraternize,
> Beware of rudely crossing it:
> I have no gun, but I can spit.[5]

The importance of this realm of experience for parapsychology lies in the fact that many psi occurrences involve meaningful perceptions or behaviour. The Realm of Meaningful Behaviour uses personal, not geometric, space. How does (or should) this influence our approach to human interactions involving Type B rather than Type A perceptions?

Perhaps the first point to make in this exploration is the fact that although the thickness of the layers of personal space with which we surround ourselves is usually quite stable, they are very flexible under certain conditions. Thus, for Americans, for example, intimate space is usually the first two feet or so from our skin. If I am in love with someone and we are separated by fourteen feet in a crowded room, and something happens in the room that has special meaning to both of us (e.g., the orchestra starts to play 'our song'), if our eyes meet, then for a moment we are each in the private space of the other. A two-foot 'surround' of each of us has expanded across the room. Conversely, if I am in social space with a group (usually, for Americans, from five to twelve feet) and their opinion makes me angry, I change them to public space and start to lecture them. In Gardner Murphy's important words, '*what is close together in psychological space is not necessarily close together in physical space, and vice versa*'[6] [italics mine].

We observe Type B perceptions in the realm of experience in which the only valid definition of space is 'psychological' or 'personal' space. This realm, the Realm of Meaningful Behaviour, is the one in which people respond to these perceptions. Yet our experiments and theories have almost consistently been designed with the definition of space used – and valid for – the sensory realm. It would be expected that with this sort of fundamental error in our planning, our results would be of the sporadic and erratic nature that they are. 'Thus far,' wrote J. B. Rhine, 'there is no relationship found between ESP scoring and time any more than between ESP scoring and space.'[7] This is what one would expect with irrelevant definitions of both 'space' and 'time'.

We do not, at present, know a great deal about proxemics and about how individuals' relationships to each other are influenced by, and influence, the personal space we place them in. Virtually all we do know is that communication is quite different in the different layers of personal space. (For example, Hall observes: 'Vocalization at the intimate distance plays a very minor part in the communication process.'[8]) What we *can* say at this point is that any psi research that involves more than one person (as in telepathy experiments) and deals with the space between them as if it were geometric space and not personal space is seriously distorting the situation and omitting a major variable. Machines interact through geometric space. Humans do not.

The viewpoint I am advancing here concerns one aspect of a proposal strongly advanced by Gardner Murphy forty years ago. He repeatedly begged parapsychologists to consider the conception that psi events should not be viewed under the old communication model that A has information, encodes it, and sends it to B, who decodes it. He suggested instead that we view them as occurrences in a dynamic field. He pointed out that:

> The old idea that the ESP process is like TV or radio transmission where the ESP target produces a signal which is picked up by the percipient, has contributed nothing to the understanding and control of ESP. Instead of conceiving of ESP as a transmission of information between individuals and objects which are otherwise distinct, Murphy pictured psi occurring within the same inter-personal field.[9]

William Roll, in an excellent recent paper,[10] has shown the importance of Murphy's field theory approach. In this approach, Murphy points out clearly that psi events take place in 'psychological' space and not in geometric space, and that psychological space can only be dealt with in terms of a dynamic field.

We have, in parapsychology, pointedly avoided any follow-up of Murphy's field theory concepts. There are a number of obvious reasons for this. As a culture, we are very spatially oriented (20 per cent of the words listed in the *Pocket Oxford Dictionary* refer to spatial qualities[11]) and are firmly committed to the idea that there is only one valid meaning to the term 'space'. Space is empty and geometric. Further, as the ecologist Garrett Hardin has said, the social sciences took their world-view from the view they perceived in physics. This 'sees the world as composed of isolated atomic units with no real relations to another . . . [except] mere side-by-side juxtaposition and eternal bumpings'.[12]

We, as parapsychologists, have committed ourselves to this concept which fits very well the sensory reality, but *does not fit at all the realms in which we observe psi events;* the Realm of Consciousness and the Realm of Meaningful Behaviour. It seems extremely likely that the design of our theoretical concepts and our experiments with the use of an inapplicable model of space are major reasons why our rate of progress in this field has been so dismal.

One of the problems of psi research has been the model of human interaction we have been using. We have been working with a model from information theory rather than the modern model of communication theory.

> [An] assumption or belief inherent in the communication paradigm . . . [of ESP] is that each person is an individual related to other individuals primarily through his messages . . . we do things to each other by means of our messages. Messages are causes which have effects. Communication study simply borrowed the Newtonian paradigm.[13]

This Newtonian model − independent entities affect each other through direct contact (messages) − is a far cry from the field theory viewpoint Murphy advocated so strongly. And this field theory approach is the modern model of communication theory.

When Ray Birdwhistell began to develop the field of non-verbal communication, he found that the concepts of communication he had expected to be able to use simply did not work; they were not applicable to use (A encodes a message – in words or gestures – and B perceives and decodes it); they could not be used to make his data lawful. He found that he had to use a very different model of non-verbal communication:

> A process that had a structure which could be found only by examining both or all of the participants in the communication process as a single unit. Communication was now a matter of dynamic relationships rather than cause-effect events. At last communication research had begun to escape the control of Newtonian cause-effect paradigm.[14]

It is time we realized the limitations of the individual-to-individual message model. It is useful in certain limited domains, including the relationships of computers to each other. In other domains of experience, such as play or ESP or face-to-face verbal and non-verbal communication, it is not very helpful. In mother-child interaction play, for example, we cannot understand what is going on in terms of messages. There is only a shared process that can only be made sense of in terms of the total unit.[15]

> The application of general system concepts to the study of inter-personal communication finally led to the long-sought breakthrough – the discovery of a basic unit of communication. The discovery emerged from the unique combination of insights derived from psychiatry, electrical and computer engineering, and general systems research. Instead of trying to analyze communication between two people as a series of discrete messages exchanged between a sender and a receiver, theorists such as Jurgen Ruesch, Gregory Bateson, David Berlo, Paul Watzlawick, Don Jackson and Virginia Satir evolved the concept of interpersonal communication as a system. When these theorists started viewing communication in this way, they discovered the concept of the basic unit of a transactional system as simply a *transaction.*
>
> In a transaction, two people are never seen as discrete elements. They are always studied in relation to each other. Within a transaction we may 'exchange messages', but the 'exchange' is largely an artificial breaking down of what is actually happening. For in reality, I do not send a message and wait for you to receive and respond to it. When you and I mutually perceive each other, we both *simultaneously* assign meanings to our behaviour. Then, with the passage of time, we modify or change the meanings.[16]

It is hard for us to realize that the modern communication model of science has changed so much and is so far from the cultural belief; that, as Byers puts it, 'the actual organization of inter-personal needs does not conform to our popular conception of human relations'. In the modern model, as Birdwhistell puts it succinctly: 'According to communication theory, John does not communicate with Mary, and Mary does not communicate with John; Mary and John engage in communication.'[17] Science no longer uses the idea that 'communication is that process by which one individual imparts information to another', except for very limited areas and for computer design.

The field theory model for psi has indeed been suggested by others who have also been ignored, particularly by those designing experiments.

> [A good analogy for ESP is not radio or lasers, but lightning] ... a sudden connection between two bodies because of the respective electric condition of these two bodies. ESP, then, could be conceived of as a kind of non-electric lightning connection bridging the gap between two meaning-related contents, contents which – if connected – prove to be complementary in regard to their meanings. In other words, the connection is the result of meaning affinity.[18]

Take this model further. The conditions of two bodies is such that a bridge is formed making a *Gestalt* of them. We now have one dynamic body. As soon as the conditions and tensions are sufficiently changed by dynamic flow within the *Gestalt,* they again become two, but a different two from what they were before. The differences may be conscious in one, non-conscious in the other, or any combination of these, but *both are changed.*

From about 1900 to the 1930s, communication research used the 'action model'. In this A sends messages to B.

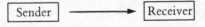

In the 1930s, this changed to the 'interactional model'. A sends a message to B, who then sends a message back.

The 'action model' and the interactional model' are the models used in information theory.

Since the 1950s, communication research has steadily moved to the modern model. In this A and B interact. What is going on can only be understood by saying that they 'engage in communication'. 'Communication is not something that one person does alone; it takes two to communicate.[19]

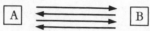

The basic unit is no longer the 'message'.[20] We now use the 'transaction', in which both are changed. Communication science has abandoned Shannon's concept of the basic unit as 'sender – message – receiver', as being of limited usefulness.[21] Communication is now described instead as 'the behaviour and experience of organisms involved in creating meaning'.[22] This immediately differentiates human and machine 'communication'. The model we have designed for our card guessing experiments is built on the older 'action' model, which includes machine-to-machine inter-action. In all probability this has been one reason for our confusion and lack of theoretical clarity.

> The action and interaction models of interpersonal communica-tion were concerned primarily with the relationship between messages and information. Meaning was of little concern and was necessarily excluded from consideration in cybernetics and information theory. The transactional approach moves the emphasis from information back to meaning.[23]

> We must consider communication in its context. For out of context the communication makes no sense. The paralysis of the rifle arm of a soldier is meaningful within the context of battle. The same behaviour isolated in the laboratory makes little sense. We cannot experiment with the soldier's behaviour; we cannot reproduce the conditions of the trauma that led to the soldier choosing hysteria as his means of communication; we do not have the capability in our laboratories of blocking all other channels of communication. As scientists we must look to the individual in his or her real life context and, like Freud, draw upon all of our scientific knowledge to make sense out of what we observe.[24]

The use of information theory in the study of psi is in many ways similar to studying life in a dead organism. We can learn a great many minor and subsidiary facts about the process, but not the essential ones. Many of the most important aspects of the situation do not apply, are outside of the concepts we are using to study the matter. How many 'bits' of information, for example, are there in a Beethoven sonata? Is there a different number when played by Schnabel or by Rubinstein? Certainly the effect on us is different.

Further, in spite of all our efforts to change the situation experimentally, consciousness is made up of processes, not of things. Processes that never repeat themselves. Information theory is simply not built to deal with this type of material.[25]

In modern communication studies (see particularly Byers[26] and Hall[27]) it has become clear that when two (or more) people communicate, they are acting in rhythm – there is a transaction going on in which each adapts their natural rhythm of action to a shared one. They act in 'synchrony' with each other. What looks ordinarily like the procedure we think of as common sense – that is, one person encodes a message in speech or action, sends it to another, who decodes it and responds to it – becomes something else again when we examine in detail what is going on. For example, in one of Byers' films, there are three people being filmed by a hidden camera – an older man, an older woman, and a young woman. The older two are talking. The younger woman crosses her legs; the man turns his head and looks at the young woman's legs. This seems entirely straightforward and simple until we examine the film frame by frame. We then find that in *the same frame* the woman starts to cross her legs and the man starts to turn his head. There are sixteen frames per second, so we know we are not dealing with the *reactions* of one person to another, but *a shared action.* The basic unit of modern communication theory is no longer the 'message', but the transaction. This is not composed of two pieces of behaviour. It is *one* piece of behaviour; each participant contributes a part. Communication is now seen as conjoint activity by two or more individuals acting in synchrony. In Ray Birdwhistell's words:

> Communication is . . . a system of interactions with a structure independent of the behaviour of the individual participant. One person does not 'communicate' with another, he engages in communication with him.[28]

Louisa Rhine made an intensive and long-term analysis of our knowledge of the parapsychology field. She found that analyzing the motivation and behaviour of the 'sender' or that of the 'receiver', 'does not yield useful information'. Dealing with Type B perception as a 'message', 'we can go no further'.[29] No matter how hard she tried, she said, 'as yet, however, no method has been found to trace the source of psi'. She could not trace it to the sender, the receiver, or even to the experimenter.

The need for the modern systems theory of communication is clear. It has not been used in parapsychology, which has continued to use the older model. There are many implications of this development in communication theory for our research in parapsychology. For example, we can no longer think of the agent communicating with the percipient. We shall have to think of them communicating with each other, and design our theories and experiments accordingly. As Byers has put it: 'Communication is a structured enterprise which requires the participation of more than one person. In this sense it is like tennis, chess or ballroom dancing.'[30]

This new viewpoint forces us to clearly differentiate the exchange of information between two computers and between two humans. The computers do not communicate, they simply transmit information from one to the other. Human beings 'entrain' their action patterns with each other, form a *Gestalt* and then separate into two individuals, different now from what they were before the 'entrainment'. These are two very different kinds of activity. Much confusion has resulted from our frequent failure to recognize this.

7
ARE PARANORMAL OCCURRENCES IMPOSSIBLE?

It is of course the merest truism that all our experimental knowledge and our understanding of nature is impossible and non-existent apart from our mental processes.

P. W. Bridgman

It is the theory which decides what we can observe.

Einstein

Whatever is fact was first in theory.

Goethe

Let us pause to see where our exploration has taken us so far.

Impossible events do not occur. Therefore, if a scientist is faced with the fact that an impossible event has occurred – the daily fare of parapsychologists – the paradox must be resolved. This *can only be done* by redefining reality in such a way that what was previously impossible now becomes possible. If the theory must bow to the brute fact, we must be clear as to what is the theory and what is the fact. Our definition of reality, which decides for us what is possible and what is impossible, is the theory. The laboratory experiment or spontaneous occurrence in which the paranormal event was demonstrated is the fact.

This is an absolutely critical point in the study of the paranormal; a point that has, in the past, received scant attention from parapsychologists. The question is – where do we get our knowledge of what is possible, and of what is impossible and therefore

115

paranormal? We have ignored the point that a definition of 'paranormal' comes from a definition of reality, *and that such a definition is a theory, not a fact.*

The opposite view, that our definition of reality is a fact and that we *know* what reality is and how it works, is a view that would make both science and philosophy tautological, as they are both a questioning and exploring of reality. Technology uses common sense; it is an accepting of a particular view of reality to accomplish our ends. Science, as Robert Oppenheimer once put it, uses uncommon sense; it is a search for new definitions and understandings. Technology takes the locally accepted definition of reality as a fact; science takes it as a theory.

Parapsychologists, in their search for acceptance as scientists, have uncritically adopted what they believed to be the scientific view of reality. They have thus, from the viewpoint of this definition, made themselves into technologists, not scientists.

The kind of uncommon sense, of daring and questioning of basic definitions needed in science, the kind we need in parapsychology, is shown by a remark of the great German mathematician David Hilbert (1862-1943). He had once mentioned a new student of his who seemed to show great promise. Some time later the philosopher Ernst Cassirer asked him what happened to this student. Hilbert replied, 'Oh he did not have enough imagination to be a mathematician so he became a poet.'[1]

The tendency of parapsychologists has been to hold their imagination in check and to accept the common, everyday definition of reality that made the facts they observed in their work impossible. Only occasionally have they been aware that this definition was a theory, not a fact.

The viewpoint of the philosopher David Hume that testimony, as to the existence of paranormal events, could never be believed, has become central to the criticisms of the data of psychical research, and to our doubts about our own work as we labour in the field. Hume put it quite simply: 'A miracle is a violation of the laws of nature. The only sufficient testimony for it would be testimony whose falsehood would be even more miraculous than the miracle itself.'[2]

Since, in Hume's terms, a 'law of nature' has infinite reliability (it is not a theory, it is a fact), it would take testimony of *more than infinite* reliability to disprove it. By definition, this is impossible, and therefore so are 'miracles'. The argument, 'In trying to prove the truth of precognition [in this case the auguries] you are overturning the whole system of physics', was first stated, to my knowledge, by Cicero in a letter to his brother Quintus.[3]

In another statement of his viewpoint, Hume wrote: 'A miracle is a violation of the laws of nature: and as a firm and unalterable experience has established these laws, the proof against a miracle, from the very nature of the fact, is as entire as any argument from experience can possibly be imagined.'[4] Or, in Thomas Paris's summation of Hume's point of view: 'Is it more likely that nature should go out of her course or that a man should lie?'

Hume was in error in this famous argument on disbelief in miracles, and similarly the countless arguments against parapsychology stemming from it are in error. The error lies in the fact that Hume defined his interpretation of how-the-world-works as a fact when it was a theory. As a *fact*, and given the faith of philosophy and science in the consistency of reality, it was blatantly impossible for it to be contradicted by another fact (the paranormal occurrence), and therefore the paranormal occurrence logically never happened, and the observers were either mistaken or lying. The chain of logic is unassailable so long as the definition remains unquestioned. Once, however, the definition is examined, it becomes clear that it is a theory, not a fact, and that when opposed by a fact it must be given up as inaccurate or incomplete.

We can see the problem clearly when we think about the colleagues of Galileo who refused to look through the telescope. They refused because it was unnecessary to look; they had confused their theory about reality with facts. As far as they were concerned, they knew the facts and there was simply no point in observing a contradictory fact; the telescope's view was necessarily false because it contradicted known facts. At this distance we can see their reasoning and their confusion clearly. It is, however, harder to see when the modern scientist, not looking at the facts of parapsychology, simply dismisses them as necessarily false and therefore unnecessary to examine, since – for him – they contradict a known fact. He is as confused as Galileo's contemporaries, but it is a lot harder to see close up.

This example raises a question concerning one aspect of Type B perceptions about which it is important to be clear. Do these perceptions, or psi occurrences in general, *contradict* any of the known and clearly established laws in science? It is widely believed that they do. By and large, it has been accepted that they violate laws well established by long and hard scientific endeavour: laws that we *know* are valid. The reasoning of many serious and trained scientists has thus been that the psi occurrences simply cannot have happened.

However, no one seems to be clear about exactly *which* laws would be violated by such occurrences. A letter by the physicist Henry Margenau and the present author, submitted to the journal *Science,* is relevant here.

It appears to be a matter of common sense to any scientifically trained person today that ESP (telepathy, clairvoyance, precognition) is impossible, since such phenomena − if they existed − would violate known and proven scientific laws. On this basis we can confidently predict that reports of occurrences of this kind are due to poor observation, bad experimental design, or outright chicanery. Old wives' tales and pretentious occultism even if dressed up in pseudo-experimental designs, do not belong in scientific journals unless studied as psychological and anthropological phenomena.

This is the attitude of many modern scientists and appears to most of us to be completely reasonable. Further, there is little question that a goodly number − at least − of reports of ESP are due to the aforementioned infelicities.

However, a question can be raised as to exactly what scientific laws would be violated by the occurrence of ESP. We have assumed that they are of the stature of the Law of Conservation of Energy and Momentum, the Second Law of Thermodynamics, the principle of causality, and the exclusion principle of quantum mechanics. When we examine scientific laws of this calibre, however, we find them unrelated to the existence or non-existence of ESP.

Further, as concerns conservation of energy, physics itself tolerates curious exceptions, or at any rate, it considers phenomena which alter the usual conception of this basic principle. The equivalence of mass and energy modifies its classical meaning; the need for introducing 'negative kinetic energy states', together with holes in their distribution which represent particles, extends its scope immensely and dilutes its meaning. Electrons can pass through barriers in a way which energy conservation in old-style physics would not have permitted, and in the quantum theory of scattering, one is forced to introduce 'virtual states' which violate it.

It is indeed questionable that ESP strains the energy conserva-tion principle even as much as these innovations do, for it is not at all certain that the transmission of information must be identified with that of energy or mass.

Does ESP violate the canon against 'action-at-a-distance?' Perhaps it would if there were such a universal principle. There are current, at present, respectable conjectures among physicists who introduce massless fields in which phenomena can be transmitted instantly. In quantum mechanics, a debate is raging about non-locality of interactions; the term is a high-brow version of action-at-a-distance, which is believed by some serious theorists to be required in order to solve the EPR paradox. ESP is no stranger than some of the discussions in this field.

Strangely, it does not seem possible to find the scientific laws or principles violated by the existence of ESP. We *can* find contradic-tions between ESP and our culturally accepted view of reality, but not — as many of us have believed — between ESP and the scientific laws that have been so laboriously developed. Unless we find such contradictions, it may be advisable to look more carefully at reports of these strange and uncomfortable phenomena which come to us from trained scientists and fulfill the basic rules of scientific research. We believe that the number of these high quality reports is already considerable and increasing.*

A theory about reality, a conception of how-the-world works, which is so real to us that we perceive and react as if it were true, as if it were a fact, can be described in two ways. From one viewpoint, it is a state of awareness, a state of consciousness, a way of being-in-the-world. From this viewpoint, the one we have when we are using the theory personally, we are responding to the truth about reality. This is how things and we are. From the other viewpoint, it is simply an integrated set of hypotheses concerning reality and is judged by its effectiveness in attaining whatever goals seem

*It may be of interest that *Science* did not respond to this letter. After three letters of inquiry no acknowledgement at all was forthcoming. A personal telephone call to the President of the American Association for the Advancement of Science, which publishes the journal, finally elicited a reply from one of the editors that our letter 'placed the burden of proof on the detractors rather than the supporters of psi', and that it had therefore been rejected. It is obvious that this comment was completely irrelevant to the letter.

relevant to whoever is doing the judging. It is a theory of metaphysics, to be compared with other theories of the same kind.

These two descriptions – a state of consciousness and a metaphysical theory – are the opposite sides of the same coin. When using them, we are talking about the same thing from two different angles. They are the same phenomena experienced in two different ways.

This has definite implications. It indicates that there is no such thing as a generally 'correct' or 'normal' state of consciousness, only various states that can be compared in the way they succeed in aiding us, permitting us, to solve our problems or arrive at our goals.

What are these problems? What are these goals? In a dream, we have a specific and coherent metaphysical theory; we are in a specific state of consciousness that is different from our ordinary twentieth-century, Western state of consciousness (the state we generally consider to be 'normal' or 'correct'). Dreaming is necessary for us; we suffer negative personality changes when it is prevented. It helps us attain some goal that we can apparently not attain (at least as well) in other known states of consciousness. We have thus two states of consciousness (waking and dreaming), each appropriate to certain of our human goals. The mystic trains himself to attain still other states, and believes that these are also essential to full human development, to the solution of certain of our needs.

From the viewpoint of modern science, the physicist takes the other side of the mystic's coin. He believes that certain theories about reality are necessary to solve some problems. Other theories are necessary to solve other problems. His theories are certainly related to, and are compatible with, each other. But for all the relationships between the theories about reality that the physicist posits as being necessary, they are very different and have very different entities and laws in them. (They demand, on the reverse side of the coin, very different states of consciousness to respond experientially to them.) What is possible in one metaphysical theory is impossible – paranormal – in another. I might point out, for example, that what is perfectly normal on a subatomic level – for an electron to jump from one 'orbit' to another without crossing the intervening space – is teleportation on a molar level and is, to say the least, paranormal. The theories about reality that the physicist posits and uses in these two realms are that different – and more.

We could find many more similar examples. As mentioned earlier, that an electron can pass through two separate holes of a plate at the same time without splitting is perfectly normal in the theory used to deal with problems on a quantum level. In the theory used in everyday life, this is bilocation – a paranormal phenomenon. In another theory about reality, the theory used by the relativity physicist, we have the normal phenomena of Event A occurring before Event B from the viewpoint of one observer, the two events occurring at the same time from the viewpoint of a second observer, and Event A occurring after Event B from the viewpoint of a third observer. It is literally impossible with many events to say whether they occurred simultaneously or in sequence. With the 'common-sense', everyday theory about reality, this would lead to precognition and retrocognition – paranormal phenomena. The theories about reality – what it is and how it works – that the physicist finds it necessary to use are so different that what is impossible and paranormal in one is frequently perfectly possible and normal in another.

When the same words are used to describe events within different metaphysical systems, they are often no more than booby traps because their meaning in each system is completely different. We learn that an 'electron' has 'spin'. 'Spin', we know, is the movement an object describes on itself, like the rotation of a planet or a top upon its axis. It is a simple, familiar concept that we can all understand. We thus come to the intuitive and clear belief that an electron is a small, round object, though it might equally be a cube or pie-shaped, that spins rapidly as it moves. But then we find out that in whatever position the observer places himself, he is always in line with the axis of rotation of the spin! It becomes clear that the word 'spin' has acquired a completely new meaning in this system. Further, we find out that our small 'round' object can have no colour or absence of colour and that it cannot have a temperature. It becomes obvious to us that our intuitive and clear understanding bears no relationship to the phenomenon of an 'electron'. (It does not even exist in the usual sense that bicycles and billiard balls exist. It has, rather, as Werner Heisenberg stated, 'a tendency to exist'.[5])

We have transposed events and terms from one metaphysical system, one way of construing reality, into another, and arrived at complete confusion.

We are led here to a revolutionary understanding. This is that a number of metaphysical systems – states of consciousness – are equally valid in any overall sense. None is closer to any 'true reality' than any other, and if it were we should never have a way of knowing this, since all we can ever perceive is reality *after* it has been construed and shaped by our consciousness; after Edmund Husserl's 'enormous a priori', the question 'Which metaphysical theory is true?' is vacuous. It cannot ever be answered. A question we can deal with, however, is, 'What can we accomplish with one metaphysical theory, and what can we accomplish with another?' Henry Margenau has stated this clearly when he wrote: 'The question, then, is not whether matter is continuous, but how theories succeed when they regard as a continuum the construct which they take to be their system.[6]

(There were, the story goes, three baseball umpires who were asked how they could tell a 'strike' from a 'ball'. The first said, 'I calls them as they are.' The second said, 'I calls them as I see them.' The third, answering in accord with the viewpoint of modern science, said, 'They ain't nothing until I calls them.')

Similarly, the other side of the coin. We no longer ask 'Which state of consciousness is the correct one, so that when using it we perceive and react to reality?' The concept of a 'correct' or 'normal' state of consciousness is one we will have to put on the crowded and dusty shelf marked 'Outmoded ideas: Ingest at your own risk'. We can, however, ask such questions as: 'Which state of consciousness is most useful to solve certain needs and goals?' And 'Which state of consciousness is statistically most prevalent in which cultural situations?'

This comprehension is the most staggering and least understood insight of modern science. We no longer search for what reality is, but rather for ways of usefully construing it; ways to define it that will help us achieve our goals. We now see that there is no 'right' metaphysical system, only a number of ones of limited usefulness; that there is no 'correct' state of consciousness that will reflect 'reality', only a number of states useful or useless for specific human purposes.

The next step follows naturally. If there are a number of different, equally 'right' metaphysical systems – states of consciousness – and these are quite different in the entities and laws they contain, then we can do certain things in some of them that we cannot do in others. What is 'normal' in one of them is 'paranormal' in another. For something to be 'paranormal' in a particular construction of reality means that it is forbidden by the basic limiting principles of that construction and it does not happen when we are using it. *It cannot be 'explained' in that metaphysical theory since it does not happen in it.* One cannot explain impossible events within the metaphysical system (theory about reality) in which they are impossible.

This must be clearly understood. It is central to the problem parapsychologists have had in 'explaining' or 'understanding' psi phenomena. If a system of reality-ordering forbids certain events from occurring (such as, in our everyday system, an effect preceding its cause in time) you cannot explain that event within the system. It is like trying to explain parallel lines meeting within the system of Euclidean geometry. You can try all you want, but it simply cannot be done. If an apparently impossible event occurs (as in laboratory demonstrations of precognition) you have to explain it within a system in which it *can* occur. You can explain the parallel lines meeting within the system of Riemannian geometry: you cannot in the Euclidean system. It is not that it is difficult or complex to explain; it cannot be done.

There is an old story about the lost traveller who asked the countryman how to get to Salisbury. The farmer replied, 'You go north five miles and then turn west . . . no, that's no good. You go west three miles and take the first road north . . . no, that won't do it. You go east and then. . . . By God, you can't get there from here!' Parapsychologists have tried and tried to get from here to there on the solid-appearing roads of our ordinary theory about reality. It can't be done. In our ordinary construing of reality we can do certain things and we cannot do others. We can travel to Yankee Stadium, Waterloo Station or the Place de l'Etoile. We cannot travel to the day before yesterday or to the Land of Oz. You can perceive something with your senses or extrapolate from known data. You cannot be clairvoyant or precognitive. Certain things cannot be done and we had better learn to accept this. You cannot explain events forbidden by a system within that system. That's just the way things are and we are going to have to learn to live with it.

In bringing this revolutionary understanding of modern science to our problems in parapsychology we see that events occurring in one state of consciousness, one metaphysical system, cannot always be explained in terms of another. It is not that they are difficult or complex to explain; they *cannot* be explained. The definition of impossible (paranormal) is that, within a given system, an event not only cannot occur, it cannot be explained. Psi events, being paranormal (impossible) in our everyday common-sense meta-physical system (what I have called elsewhere the 'Sensory Reality'[7]), cannot be explained in terms of it and parapsychologists might as well stop trying to do so.

From the viewpoint of this comprehension, the spiritualists and theologians were more correct than we 'scientists' when they tried to explain paranormal events by attributing them to the actions of spirits or of God. They were taking entities from another meta-physical system to explain phenomena that could not be explained in this one.

I say that the spiritualists and theologians were 'more correct' than the parapsychologists, not that they were 'correct'. The situation is similar to that of the little boy who came home and told his mother he had won first prize in a test at school. The question asked had been, 'How many legs has a horse?' He had answered, 'Three.' When his mother asked why he had come first, he replied that all the other children had said, 'Two.'

If an event is a major violation of our theory about reality, a major revision of that theory becomes necessary. The scope of the revision has to be related to the scope of the violation. If the violation does not touch basic limiting principles, only minor changes may be indicated. The inverse-square law (that the intensity measured by a constant instrument from a source declines by the square of the distance between the measuring instrument and the source) can be modified when we invent the laser, or when we differentiate the intensity of a signal and the amount of information carried by it; but the law remains valid, even though its domain has been somewhat reduced.

We need to establish what position we are forced into by our data. Is only a small modification necessary, as in the case of the inverse-square law, or a larger one, which will say in effect, 'The old basic structuring of reality remains true and valid, but its domain is now seen as limited and in other domains different laws apply'? This is what happened to Newtonian mechanics with the advent of the Einsteinian revolution. It is also what happened to Euclidean geometry after Lobachevsky and Riemann. Euclidean geometry is still valid, but its domain has been reduced. Other equally valid geometries, with different axioms and theorems, apply in other domains and are necessary to solve other problems. In Euclidean geometry, a straight line is the shortest distance between two points. In other geometries it is not.

What sort of revision in our theories about reality is necessitated by the existence of psi events? Since, as C. D. Broad and others have shown, they violate the basic limiting principles of our theory, the revision must be a major one. Equally, however, the necessary revision must include the fact that our theory about reality *is* valid in large and important domains. We operate too effectively in most cases, predict too well what effects will follow from what causes, to suspect that our usual theory is invalid. We must beware of babies and bathwaters. Our views about reality have not been lightly arrived at and cannot be lightly discarded. The problem does not demand that we throw out our basic theory about reality, but rather that we find out how much we must reduce its domain and devise a theory to fit the new as well as the old data.

We must also beware of solipsism – the belief that I am the only person in the universe and the creator of everything and everyone in it. We can construe reality in a variety of ways, organize, perceive and react to it according to a number of different patterns; but we are still construing, organizing, perceiving and reacting to *something*.

Something is 'there'. There is more than just 'me'. The 'something' may be mysterious and – in principle – unknowable; but it is real and will only bend in a number of ways in our attempts to organize it into useful patterns. What the laws and limits of this bending are, we do not as yet know; but we can be sure that they exist. We cannot make the universe into anything we wish: we can only organize it into a number of functional patterns. If there are 437 schizophrenics in a mental hospital, this does not mean that there are 437 legitimate and valid ways or organizing reality. It simply means that there are 437 schizophrenics in that hospital.

Perhaps we must come ultimately to an understanding of reality similar to the comprehension we came to in the heredity-environment, 'nature-nurture' controversy on the development of personality. After a long period of insisting that personality was attributable mostly to nature, or mostly to nurture, we have come to the conclusion that nature sets the outside limits of possibility, but that within these the individual person is such a combination, such an integration of both, that we can never separate out how much each played in forming the end product – the person we see before us at a given time.

Radhakrishnan, in his *Eastern Religions and Western Thought,* stated this viewpoint clearly: 'The objective world exists. It is not an illusion. It is real not in being ultimate, but in being a form, an expression of the ultimate. To regard the world as ultimately real is delusion.'[8]

The only way out of the predicament posed by the occurrence of psi events is to say that our usual theory about reality is valid, but that there is *more*; that our usual theory applies in certain situations (including nearly all our everyday activities) but that there are other situations which indicate that *all* reality cannot be dealt with by this theory. We are, in science, used to this procedure. We no longer try to predict the behaviour of subatomic particles by the same cause-effect theories with which we predict the behaviour of molar masses of material. Nor do we try to predict the behaviour of molar masses moving, relative to us, at close to the speed of light, by the same ordering of reality by means of which we explain and predict the behaviour of molar masses moving, relative to us, at speeds of a few dozen or a few hundred miles per hour. We have not thrown out our usual concepts of what reality is and how it works, but rather limited them to a more restricted domain. We have said, in effect: 'They are true and valid, but there is more. And the more is very different.'

Paranormal means impossible by the laws of a particular system of construing reality in terms of our usual *theory* about what reality is. Part of this theory is that it is the *only* valid theory. As we have seen, we have had to give this up in many areas, to limit its domain. Instead of continuing to say, 'This is the true way reality is and works, it is the only valid theory and all other ways are invalid', we now say, 'This is a fruitful way to construe large parts of reality – by and large the parts that are accessible to our senses – and it is also isomorphic to a state of consciousness that enables us to achieve many of our goals.'

Faced with the paranormal events that simply could not happen in our metaphysical system, we are forced to limit the domain of this system. We have done this elsewhere in science; we must do it with psi events. There is simply nothing else to do, nowhere else to go. *Impossible events do not happen.* If they do, then your definition of impossible (and therefore your theory of reality which gives you that definition) is wrong.

Parapsychologists have demonstrated the occurrence of impossible events. We can now do one of two things. We can change our definition of what is possible and impossible (and this can only be done by limiting the domain of our usual definition of reality), or we can continue to prove the existence of these events. Perhaps if we go on proving them for long enough, someone else will point out to us that they inexorably indicate that our usual theory of reality must be limited in its validity. Perhaps this outsider will even do our work for us by showing us where and how it is limited. Or we can do the job demanded of us by our science and explore its limitations and the alternative metaphysical system (model of reality) we need to explain our data. This will necessarily lead us to exploring the state of awareness needed to permit psi events to occur, and we might finally arrive at a coherent and acceptable field of science. We have been demanding (unsuccessfully) that non-believers in psi shift their approach and start believing in impossible facts. Our real task is to so shift our *own* approach as to make the impossible facts possible, and therefore believable. We can only do this by exploring and changing our definition of reality, for it is this that decides what is possible and what is impossible.

The only groups that have accepted the idea that you must change the system of reality-ordering you are using if you wish to solve certain problems are the physicists and mathematicians. They have overcome some apparently insuperable obstacles in this way. Parapsychologists have a host of similar obstacles and can surmount them in much the same way.

If we seriously go forward to determine what new organizations of reality are demanded by psi data, we must expect to have to break with established ideas and with beliefs that have seemed self-evident. There are no sacred cows in real science and almost every idea that, in the past, humans have believed to constitute a basic truth about reality has been overthrown. Until the twentieth century, for example, every model of the universe had as a cornerstone *Natura non facit saltus* – there are no leaps in nature. This is now regarded as false.

There is, indeed, no greater bigotry and rigidity of mind than the demand that all possible knowledge should be of the same type as that with which we are already familiar, and that explanations on the horizons of our present-day knowledge have in them only the structure and elements familiar in our everyday experience.[9]

There is a large but generally ignored sign over the doorway through which all must pass who wish to enter the cathedral of science. The sign reads:

> *Dangerous and Unstable Structure*
> *Undergoing Major Renovation.*
> *May be Torn Down at any Moment*
> *For Complete Rebuilding.*

Petrarch, at the beginning of the Renaissance, wrote: 'Do not believe the common statement that there is nothing new under the sun and that nothing new can be said. True, Solomon and Terence said that; but since their time, how much is new?'

If this were true in Petrarch's time, how much more true is it in ours?

So far in this book, there has been a good deal of criticism, both explicit and implicit, of the present-day science of parapsychology and of the methods it has used to study and understand Type B perceptions. To be of any real value, criticisms should be accompanied by positive suggestions. In Chapters 8 and 11, I discuss two research programmes that I believe have value.

The first, described in Chapter 8, presents a model research programme that has not, as yet, been carried out. It shows how the methods of modern science can lead to testable hypotheses concerning molar and meaningful Type B perceptions. Chapter 9 discusses one implication of this chapter and of the book so far.

Chapter 11 reports on a research programme in psychic healing, a large part of which has already been successfully completed. Through the use of the approaches described in this book, it has become possible to teach a large number of individuals to use a psychic ability in a practical manner.

The purpose of these chapters is to demonstrate that the

approach to Type B perceptions taken in this book can lead to useful scientific research programmes.

8
TYPE B PERCEPTIONS AND HUMAN RELATIONSHIPS: A MODEL OF A RESEARCH PROGRAMME[1]

In 1930, a one-eyed pilot named Hinchliffe was attempting the first East-West transatlantic flight. He had intended to fly alone. Unexpectedly, at the last moment, his financial sponsor insisted on a woman co-pilot. Several hundred miles away, on an ocean liner, unaware that Hinchliffe was making the crossing attempt at this time, or that there were any plans for anyone to be with him, two old friends of his, Air Force Colonel Henderson and Squadron Leader Rivers Oldmeadow, were in bed. In the middle of the night, Henderson, in his pyjamas, opened the door of Oldmeadow's cabin and said:

> 'God, Rivers, something ghastly has just happened. Hinch has just been in my cabin. Eye-patch and all. It was ghastly. He kept repeating over and over again, "Hendy, what am I going to do? What am I going to do? I've got the woman with me and I'm lost. I'm lost." Then he disappeared in front of my eyes. Just disappeared.'

It was during that very night that Hinchliffe's plane crashed and he and the woman co-pilot were killed.[2]

This is the type of data that historically has been the primary concern of psychical research. The information that Henderson reported was both meaningful and important. Unfortunately, very little progress has been made in the past hundred years to increase our understanding of this type of phenomenon.

In trying to understand the reason for this it may help to summarize what has been said so far concerning the processes of

130

those sciences that have made clear advances in prediction (and control where this is relevant)[3] of the data in their fields of inquiry. In these sciences we find certain identical patterns of action. These include:

1. A certain 'domain' of experience is chosen for study. This is a particular cross-section of experience of 'what is'. For example, one domain would be that of a flat, two-dimensional universe. We would call the science that studies this domain 'plane geometry'.

2. In each domain there are certain 'observables'. These are entities or processes that can either be directly observed or inferred. In the domain of the flat, two dimensional universe, there would be points, distances, angles, areas and shapes.

3. Some observables are defined in terms of others. Some, more elementary, are defined by the processes we use to perceive and to measure them, or to determine their presence or absence in a particular situation. Essentially, we define 'distance' (in many domains) by a procedure involving a ruler or a piece of string.[4]

4. In the study of these observables, the important question asked by science is: 'What are the relationships of these observables to each other?' Science does *not* ask the metaphysical question, 'What *are* these observables?' It studies rather how they vary in relation to each other; more precisely, to the degree of presence of the other observables in this domain. Thus, we do not ask, 'What is a point?' or 'What is a line or an area?' We ask rather, 'How does area vary with variations in line and angle?' 'What are the laws defining these relationships?' In another domain, we do not ask, 'What is gravity?'[5] but rather 'What are the laws defining the force with which masses attract one another?'

5. It is accepted as axiomatic that all observables in a particular domain will relate lawfully to each other. This is a basic axiom of science – that the cosmos is orderly. Although this is a clear foundation stone of modern science, there are areas in which its implications have not been clearly seen. These areas include psychical research. However, in a domain such as thermo-dynamics, we are perfectly clear that if – at a particular time in the development of the field – we do not completely understand the relationships between volume, temperature and pressure, there are still such lawful relationships.

6. Observables, and the laws relating them, are very different in different domains. Nevertheless, they are compatible. If they contradict each other, something is wrong in the analysis. This again is an aspect of the basic faith of science in the orderliness of the universe.

These propositions are widely accepted in the scientific community and are well known to its members. We are attempting here to explore one aspect of their implications for the study of Type B perceptions.

For the purposes of this chapter, we will define a psi-occurrence as *the detected possession of information held by an individual who could not have acquired this information by means of the senses or by the extrapolation of information gained by sensory means.*

Ehrenwald, in an important paper,[6] recently differentiated two types of psi-occurrence. The first refers to 'psychologically significant and dynamically meaningful incidents... of a purposeful, goal-oriented nature'. They are *need-determined.* (There is a *need* to communicate and 'ordinary' sensory communication is blocked.) The information in the experience is perceived as being important and significant to the 'receiver'.

The second type occurs without conscious awareness. It is 'structurally rather than dynamically determined ... [and] due to a cluster of neurons caught napping at their jobs, or to the irregular firing of others'. It is *flaw-determined,* due to a temporary and local breakdown of the 'filter' system that keeps us from being overwhelmed by psi-transmitted information. It is 'facilitated by such minus functions of the ego as REM sleep, relaxation, sensory deprivation, etc.' The information is erratic and not perceived by the individual consciously, or – if its existence is pointed out – the content is seen as unimportant. It is not psychologically significant to the individual.

These two types appear to be overlapping areas of a spectrum rather than clearly and sharply separate types of psi. Louisa Rhine, in her long and careful study of spontaneous cases, found the same two types described by Ehrenwald – need-determined and flaw-determined.[7]

We shall be concerned here with Ehrenwald's 'significant', 'need-determined' type of psi-occurrence. An example of this is the Hinchliffe-Henderson story quoted at the beginning of this chapter. It is this type of occurrence that has classically been of central interest in psychical research. However, in the attempt to become 'scientific' – the shift in emphasis, typified by the change from 'psychical research' to 'parapsychology' – it was widely felt that this type of occurrence should be abandoned in favour of Ehrenwald's 'flaw-determined', 'leakage' type. Typical of this concentration was the tremendous number of statistical studies of card-guessing experiments. A good deal of progress has been made in recent years in studying this second type of phenomenon.[8] Very little progress, if any, however, has been made in the study of the 'need-determined type'.[9]

Perception (both Type A and Type B) is *always* in context, and is affected by context. A recent study in *Science* showed that subjects could perceive a given letter as part of a word faster than they could perceive it in isolation. If 'coin' and 'join' were very rapidly flashed on a screen, the subjects identified them more rapidly (at a shorter flashed interval) than they did 'c' or 'j' as a single letter.[10]

This is hardly a new insight. The Roman Sextus Empiricus wrote: 'The vestibule of the bath house warms those who enter from the street, and chills those leaving the baths ... the same wine seems sour to those who have eaten dates, and sweet to those who have eaten nuts.[11]

An old idea it is, but one which psychology and parapsychology have long ignored. It is only recently that we are beginning to recognize its crucial nature for our understanding.

In this context, Louisa Rhine, summing up her vast experience with spontaneous ESP cases, wrote:

> By means of these experiences, the person gets information about the world, but this information is *definitely slanted to his own interests and viewpoint* ... the potential range of material accessible to ESP is as wide – but no wider than – the personal interests of the individual through whom it is expressed [author's italics].[12]

The point here is that human interest and perception is the same in both the sensory and paranormal domains; it is an ego-centred, *personal* matter. R. A. McConnell wrote: 'The *sine qua non* of ESP is a psychological relationship – preferably an emotion-laden relationship – between the percipient and the source of his information.'[13] After an intensive analysis of psi-occurrences Ian Stevenson concluded: 'a *relationship,* not just an individual, is necessary for such experiences to occur'.[14]

Let us take one more example of this type of psi-occurrence, of Type B perception:

> Rosalind Heywood, a psychic, and a very serious student of Psychic Research, was living in London in 1964 with her husband, Frank. She lived in Wimbledon, a suburb, and he worked in town. On this particular day, he had driven into London in the morning and was expected home at around 6 p.m. At about 2 p.m. she began to have a very strong feeling that she had to be at the railroad station (about one and a half miles from her home) by 3 o'clock. (She had frequently had psi-occurrences of this form – a strong compulsion which she called her 'orders' – happen to her before.) She went to a neighbour's house to borrow the neighbour's car, but it was in a garage being repaired. She went to a second neighbour's house and borrowed a car there. She arrived at the railroad station at 3 o'clock, just in time to meet Frank, who had suddenly, and with no warning, become ill in the city. It was his first heart attack and he had no idea what was happening to him. He felt too ill to drive home, and took the train. He realized too late – after he was on the train – that he should have gone to a London hospital or, at the least, phoned Rosalind to meet him, but he had been too sick to think clearly. He got off the train very ill; she drove him directly to the hospital. Later, the physicians told them that it was only due to his being treated in time that he had survived.

To begin the approach we are suggesting here, let us decide on the realm of experience with which psychical research is concerned. This is the cross-section of experience in which there is more than one human being. Simply put, it is in this domain in which we *observe* psi-occurrence. (Further, although it appears possible to conceive of pure clairvoyance or precognition in a one-person cosmos, it calls for a great deal of intellectual stretching. More important, however, is the fact that it is almost impossible to conceive of a person, a human being, developing or existing as such, alone in the universe. If, as W. Köhler once wrote: 'A solitary chimpanzee is not a chimpanzee,' how much more obviously true is this of a solitary human being? A voluminous literature in psychology and psychiatry bears clear witness that human psychological characteristics only develop in the working out of relationships with other persons.)

In this domain – of multiple human beings – we find three

relevant classes of observables 'appearing'. They are 'self-aware individual identity', 'communication', and 'relationships between people'. There may well be other observables we will wish to include later, but these will suffice for the present. If we wish to follow the classical model of the successful sciences, our primary question will be: 'How do these observables relate to one another?' We will find ways to define our terms carefully as we proceed. For the purpose of demonstrating the possibility of this scientific model for psychical research, however, we can be content for the time being with doing this in a general and rather loose way. 'Communication' we will define for now as the detectable transmission of information between two individuals. We shall divide this into two kinds: sensory communication, in which the transmission takes place through the sensory organs or through manipulation of information that was acquired in this way; and Type B, non-sensory communication or psi-occurrences. We are (following Honorton) inserting a 'detectable' into both of these definitions, since non-detectable entities or processes are of no interest to science. (It may well be, for example, that psi transmission of information always or usually accompanies sensory transmission of the identical information. However, this, if true, would not be detectable and science takes it as a general operating rule that entities that are – in principle – non-detectable are to be treated as if they do not exist. See, for example, the history of the concept of the 'ether'.)

Psi-occurrences are only detectable when sensory communication between those involved is blocked. For our purposes, then, psi occurs when sensory communication is blocked. Since our interest here is in the 'need-determined' type of occurrence, there obviously must also be a need to communicate on the part of at least one of the persons involved.

Let us now begin to make hypotheses as to what the relationships are between these three observables – communication, relationships and identity. So far as communication is concerned, we are interested, as already indicated, in that type that occurs when information transmission through sensory systems is blocked and there is a need to communicate. Such communication – Ehrenwald's 'need-determined' type – are of important events, important at least to one of the individuals concerned.

Let us look first at the observable 'relationship'. Do we already know anything about this that can be of help in formulating testable hypotheses? It turns out there is a good deal that we already know. From the research into small group behaviour, for example from the Group Dynamics of Kurt Lewin and his students, and from the Interaction Process Analysis of R. F. Bayles and his followers, we can make some definite statements. (It should be borne in mind that the 'small group' starts with and includes the dyad – two people relating to each other.)

There is, for example, a measurable attribute in relationships generally called 'cohesion'. This has been defined as 'the total field of forces which acts on members to remain in the group[15]; or, in a dyad, to continue the relationship. A great deal of research has been devoted to this factor. (An observable in science may have attributes – as the observable 'force', in physics, has the attributes 'strength' [as measured in number of dynes] and 'direction'. 'Cohesion' is analogous to the attribute 'strength of force' in physics.)

Using 'cohesion' as the dependent variable, the following conditions are among those which have been shown to affect it:

A. Cohesion is greater when the emphasis in the group has been on co-operation rather than competition.

B. Cohesion is greater in a democratically organized group than it is in a group governed by authoritarian or *laissez-faire* procedures.[16]

Our first hypothesis, then, might be that *psi-occurrences are more frequent between individuals whose relationships have been co-operative than they are between individuals whose relationships have been competitive.* Our second hypothesis might be that *psi-occurrences are more frequent in egalitarian than in authoritarian groups.* Although testing these hypotheses would be difficult and would require various 'correction factors' for bias, the tests themselves seem perfectly feasible.

Since the stronger the interpersonal attractions among its members, the greater the group cohesion,[16] we can make a third hypothesis: *psi-occurrences are more frequent between people who like each other than between people who do not.* It is of interest that recent studies by Carl Sargent and by Gertrude Schmeidler have shown that parapsychologists who get good experimental results are more likely to be more open, warm and friendly than those who do not.[17]

The reasoning behind the above hypotheses is not complex. The greater the cohesion of a relationship or a group, the greater will be the tendency to continue communication in the face of difficulty. The blockage of sensory communication is one such difficulty. Psi-occurrences of the type here under consideration may be conceptualized as a way of continuing communication when sensory channels are blocked. Therefore, whatever increases group cohesion will increase the predicted frequency of the occurrences. There are known to be other testable variables that affect cohesion as well as direct measures of cohesion. We could thus make other predictions of the above kind. These three examples, however, should suffice to demonstrate this possibility for present purposes.

From the research on the observable 'communication' we have data indicating that important interpersonal transmissions of information (transmissions that change the persons involved in a way that is perceived by at least one of them to be significant) tend to take place between individuals identifying themselves as members of the same group.[18] We would therefore make the following hypothesis: *people who identify themselves as members of the same, important (to them) group, will report psi-occurrences between them more frequently than those who do not.*

Social class in the United States is a system that tends to separate individuals into different groups, life-styles and patterns. The individual's position in the social class structure is generally determinable. We might therefore make the following hypothesis: *psi-occurrences between two members of different social classes will be reported much less frequently than between members of the same social class. (This, however, will not be true if there exists a special group that includes both of them and is important to at least one of them.)* The implication of these two hypotheses for the psychological design of psi experiments and behaviour of laboratory staff is obvious.

Bayles[19] and others of his school have approached communication primarily from the viewpoint of problem-solving activity. They demonstrate, for example, in a large number of experiments, that human beings need and strive for stability (another attribute of the observable 'relationship') in their dealings with others and develop 'roles' to maintain this stability. Solutions to problems of interaction become institutionalized as roles so that stability (and therefore predictability) can exist. (There are also, of course, other reasons for the development of roles.) Bayles has demonstrated the consistency and importance of this aspect of relationships.

A 'role' can be approached from both a sociological aspect ('He is a father to those children') and from a psychological aspect ('He is a very demanding father'). There is a strong tendency for roles in a group (including a dyad) to be consistent and for communications to be relevant to them.[19] We might, therefore, make the following hypothesis: *a psi-occurrence will be in keeping, both sociologically and psychologically with the role that the 'agent' plays or has played in relation to the 'percipient'.*

If Rosalind Heywood had worked out a relationship with her husband in which she never took care of him when he was sick, it would be very unlikely – according to this hypothesis – that the reported incident would have taken place. Either she would have received other 'orders' in keeping with her role in relation to him, someone else would have been involved in the psi-occurrence, or it would not have happened at all. If Henderson and Oldmeadow – in the example given at the beginning of this chapter – had not been the old war comrades and superiors whom Hinchliffe would have been likely to turn to in case of trouble in the air, they would not have had this particular Type B perception.

A second hypothesis might be that *psi-occurrences are more likely when the stability of an important relationship is threatened and communication is necessary to maintain it, but when sensory modes of communication are blocked.*

In his work, Bayles has developed a method of analyzing verbal communications in a relationship into four general classes: Positive Reactions, Attempted Answers, Questions, and Negative Reactions.[19] The first three classes indicate that the predominant forces operating under these circumstances are those favouring the continuance of the relationship, the fourth indicates a desire to discontinue it. In terms of our earlier comments about cohesion, we might make the hypothesis that *verbal communications preceding psi-occurrences are more frequent in the first three classes than in the fourth* (again, with necessary correction factors in the research design).

These hypotheses are concerned with the mutual variations between the observables 'relationship' (specifically, its attributes of cohesion and stability) and 'communication'. The same type of hypotheses can be made concerning the variation between psi-occurrences (the type of 'communication' we are interested in here) and 'identity'.[20]

The interactions between relationship and identity have been widely explored in a large number of contexts within scientific, artistic and literary frameworks. It has long been clear that one cannot exist without the other and it does not seem necessary here to describe and cite the extremely voluminous literature which is unanimous on this point.[21] Further, it has become clear that although there may be shorter or longer periods in the individual's life when direct communication is cut off (the Robinson Crusoe situation, for example), the three observables of identity, communication and relationship are as interdependent as are volume, pressure and temperature in another domain.[22] It is the consciousness of a relationship or membership of a group that is important in determining identity and behaviour. 'Groups have a consciousness of membership which may, indeed, persist even when intercourse with co-members has ceased, as with an Englishman living abroad.'[23]

Let us here use as one aspect of the observable 'identity' Erik Erikson's definition: identity is the ability to maintain important patterns in the face of change.[24]

Since the evidence from the literature demonstrates that the individual strives to maintain his identity with the same intensity and need as he does to maintain his relationships, we can make certain hypotheses about the interaction of 'identity' and the frequency of psi-occurrences. One example of this would be: *the psi-occurrence will tend to aid the individual in maintaining important patterns in the face of change.* In other words: *psi-occurrences will tend to stabilize identity and maintain consistency of action and perception more often than they will tend to destabilize identity.*

All the hypotheses presented so far seem to have much in common. This is because we are dealing with a *Gestalt*[25] of identity, communication and relationships. To be sure, separating them is artificial and is done only for the purposes of making the hypotheses testable. Ernst Cassirer has pointed out, for example, that a major function of language is to ensure that a group has a common experience of reality, and that the participants are enabled to communicate, relate and maintain their identities.[26]

At the beginning of this chapter, I made the point that those sciences which had been able to make definite progress in the past had followed courses containing similar steps and procedures. These included *the selection of a specific domain, the identification and definition of the observables in this domain, and a concentration on the question of the relationships between these observables.* In the history of psychical research, it was not believed possible to do this with certain types of data. These types included the meaningful, 'need-determined' psi-occurrences.[27]

Scientific procedures in the field, therefore, focused primarily on the less personally meaningful type of psi-occurrence that Ehrenwald has labelled 'flaw-determined'. Methods have been developed by Rhine and his followers, to study these with careful and precise scientific procedures. We might loosely characterize the change from 'psychical research' to 'parapsychology' as being a change in emphasis from the study of mediums and of death bed apparitions to the study of Zener cards and random numbers.

My purpose here has been to demonstrate how domain theory could be applied to the field of parapsychology. In doing this I showed that a scientific approach could be made to the area of need-determined psi-occurrences, and gave some basic examples of the kinds of hypotheses that could be made and tested. The existing rich literature on relationships and on identity, as well as the extensive literature on psychologically significant psi-occurrences, gives us a wide field in which to make and test other hypotheses concerning this domain.

The implications of this approach are many. They lead, for example, to hypotheses as to what kind of information may be expected to be transmitted in this type of occurrence.[28] It also has major implications for the problem of epistemological feedback, in this context often called 'experimenter effect', and how to deal with it in experimental situations, as well as for a number of other problems in the field.

I should like to illustrate the approach outlined so far by three case histories of Type B perceptions.

> In the family of the philosopher Ernst Cassirer, a specific behaviour of his was widely known. During the years that his daughter Anna had been in boarding school, there had been three or four occasions when he had woken up in the middle of the night and insisted on telephoning to the school. On each of these occasions she had been taken sick and was in the infirmary. As she was basically a healthy child, these were rare occasions for her. He

never called in this way when she was well.

Many years later, when she was an adult, the two of them were at a party in Berlin where she was studying. The next morning, he took the express back to his home in Hamburg. There was one stop between the two cities, the town of Wittenberg. As the express pulled into this station, Cassirer took his suitcase, got off the train, went to the nearest phone booth, called Berlin and asked, 'What happened? What is the matter with Anna?' The housekeeper referred him to the hospital. An hour after he left on the train, she had suddenly begun to haemorrhage and was in emergency surgery.[29]

The second case concerns an incident that happened to my wife, Eda LeShan, during the years when I was training people in psychic healing (see Chapter 11). The following report is in her own words, as it appeared in her book *Living Your Life*.[30] I later interviewed the aunt involved and found the story completely corroborated.

I found the first years of Larry's research intellectually stimulating, and finally I decided I wanted to have the direct emotional experience of being a member of one of his workshops in California. Paranormal experiences can be facilitated by training in the art of meditation, and learning how to meditate is very tough work. This was a five-day programme, in which we worked eight to ten hours a day, trying to gain control over our minds. There is nothing that is more difficult than doing just one thing at a time, and that is what meditation is really all about. It is training the mind in the same way that one can train the body for better physical control through exercise or weight lifting, or playing tennis.

I didn't really expect anything to happen to me; I was too practical, too down-to-earth; too set in the everyday reality of my senses, to be able to have any sort of mystical experience. All the rational humanism of my childhood was too deeply ingrained for me to make the leap into any sort of altered state of consciousness.

Much to my astonishment, after a few days of seriously trying to follow the exercises, I sensed a change taking place in myself: strange things were happening for which I could not account in my orderly scheme of things. My mind was going out of its head!

Before this seminar began in California, there had been a birthday party for my mother in New York. She'd had a heart condition for many years, but on that particular night she seemed especially happy, relaxed and loving. It was therefore a great shock to get a telephone call from my father a day or two later that she was back in the hospital, in great pain – and very frightened. My brother told me that my mother was so agitated and terrified that no amount of medication seemed to be helping – she was moaning and crying, even in her sleep. When I talked to my mother on the phone, however, she assured me there was no reason for returning to New York, that she had had such episodes before, and would recover again.

One of the exercises that Larry uses to help people begin to meditate is to have each member of the group go off by him or herself and for fifteen minutes, simply say his or her own first name over and over again, out loud. The reason for this is that we rarely hear ourselves saying our own names, and it seems to help to break down one's usual way of perceiving the world enough to allow new and different mental experiences to occur.[31] It was easy, in a beautiful forest setting, for each of us to find a place to be alone, and Larry moved from one to another to see how we were doing.

I sat down on a tree stump, closed my eyes and began saying 'Eda, Eda', over and over again, feeling how strange that sounded. After a while – I had no idea how much time had passed – Larry said it was about ten or fifteen minutes – something really weird began to happen to me. I felt as if I was moving away from the sense of being an individual sitting on a log, and that I was suddenly moving out into space – that I had become part of the total universe and that that was a safe and wonderful place to be – almost like one tiny star in a great galaxy. My first thought was that I would never again be frightened of dying, that I felt so much part of a larger universe that I could never feel lost and alone, but rather was connected forever to everything. I thought of my mother and wished in a deeper way than ever before that somehow I could share this moment with her – that I *was with her,* and that I wanted her to feel what I was feeling – this sense of deep inner peace, the Oneness with a kind of universal ALL in which she and I could never be separated, and in which there was such serenity and awe and peace.

I burst into tears. Larry appeared, and we sat quietly, and I told him what had happened to me. The exercise had taken me out of my ordinary sense of myself – I had, much to my surprise, discovered an alternative state of consciousness.

Later that day my father called to tell me my mother had died and I flew back to New York. After the funeral, at my parents' apartment, I was helping others put some food on the dining room table, when I heard my aunt telling a story to some other relatives. She was saying that my mother, in spite of the enormous amounts of medication she was getting, had been moaning and tossing restlessly, when suddenly she sat straight up in bed and said in a clear and quiet voice, 'Oh, it's so peaceful here in the forest!' She lay back in bed and slept – and died soon thereafter.

Some time later, Larry and I figured out the time difference between New York and California, and realized that the episode my aunt had described occurred at the time I had been in the altered state of consciousness.

These two cases of Type B perceptions illustrate how the roles and relationships of two people are maintained through psi-occurrences. Both experiences were consistent with the caring and protective roles that one of the persons involved had with another.

Not all Type B perceptions are as serious as the ones reported in this chapter so far. Different kinds of roles lead to different kinds of Type B perception. In the following case, we see how the role of 'Expert Psychic in a Research Situation' can lead to quite different responses. The incident reported here is one that occurred when I first started to work with Eileen Garrett, and has been written up in one of the professional journals of the field.[32] The following is the published report.

> During the course of a pilot study on fingertip vision at the Parapsychology Foundation, I – as a specialist in research design – was asked to come in and help to tighten up the experimental procedure. This was the third time I had ever met Mrs Garrett, who was the subject in the pilot study. The first two meetings had been exclusively discussions of parapsychology with no personal information talked of. However, she had seen a professional *curriculum vitae* of mine, and a colleague (Dr Ivan London) had told her that I was married and had a daughter.
>
> After discussing the pilot study procedure with Mrs Garrett and Dr Roberto Cavanna, we made an appointment for the next morning to do some test runs.
>
> That evening, thinking the matter over, I decided to try a modification in the next morning's procedure. The targets had been 4-inch cardboard squares of different colours. Knowing something of Mrs Garrett's orientation to life and nature from her books, I decided to try some targets with more 'life' in them. I obtained three identical transparent boxes and looked around for something to put in them. My daughter walked by at this moment, and I took a small lock of her hair and put it in the first box. From our backyard garden I cut a rosebud and put it in the second. Some neighbours had just moved in next door that week and, as they and their dog were then on their back porch, I asked them for a tuft of hair from their dog's tail.

The next morning (May 24, 1964) I brought the three boxes into the experimental room. Present were Mrs Garrett, Mrs Bethe Pontorno as shorthand notetaker, and myself. I told Mrs Garrett that I had decided to change the targets and showed her the three boxes one at a time. Each one – after my comments – she simply held and looked at for 10-20 seconds. My comments were as follows:

> This is a lock of hair from my daughter, Wendy.
> This is a tuft from the tail of our neighbour's
> dog. He is a purebred Welsh terrier named Charlie.
> This is a rosebud.

After this, without further conversation, I took the three boxes behind the visual screen set-up (the 'Cavanna Box' – a special screen system designed to study fingertip vision*) and put them out of sight. Mrs Garrett put her right arm through the sleeve of the screen system. I picked each box in turn (in an order determined by random number tables) and slid it beneath her fingers. Her comments were as follows:

Mrs Garrett's Comments	*Discussion*
Box 1	
'Oh, that's your daughter. I think I'll call her "Hilary". She'd like that.'	When my daughter was four years old she had a 'crush' on a girl of six named Hilary. For a year she begged us to change her name to Hilary. Nothing like this had ever happened before or since. It was a private family joke for several years thereafter that had never been – to the recollection of my wife or myself – mentioned outside the immediate family. It had certainly *not* been mentioned in at least four years by any of us.

*The 'Cavanna Box' was designed for studying 'dermal vision' by Dr Roberto Cavanna. It is a five-sided box about 2 feet by 1½ feet by 1½ feet. It is electrically lit from inside and is open on the side facing the experimenter. The side facing the subject has a hole in it, circular, about 5 inches in diameter; attached to the hole is a sleeve, about 20 inches long, of heavy, double black cloth. The subject thrusts an arm through the sleeve and thus can touch objects which he cannot possibly see visually.

'She should ride horses. There is something between her and horses. They understand each other.'

This is true. My daughter rides like a cavalry officer and can gentle the most upset horse. However, many girls of her age enjoy horseback riding and are very interested in it. An estimate of my daughter's approximate age could have been easily made intuitively from my age or from the lock of hair.

'She has a special relationship with her father. She loves her mother, but is particularly close to her father at this time.'

True, but this is valid for a very large number of girls of her approximate age.

'She is nice. She's better and more interested in art and literature than the sciences.'

This is true. (I certainly believe she is a 'nice' person.) The 'interest' statement is true but rather general. It could apply to many people.

'She has been very interested in American History these past few weeks, hasn't she?'

Three weeks before my daughter had been given an English assignment in school to do a book review of Howard Fast's book on the American Revolution, *April Morning*. For the first time in her life she became interested enough in a subject to go to the school library and ask for more books about it. During these last three weeks she had read several other books on the American revolution and the period, Fast's *Conceived in Liberty*, *Johnny Tremain* by Esther Forbes, and others. She was fascinated by the subject during that time. To the strong belief of my wife and myself, this was not mentioned outside the house, although her teachers and school friends may have known of it.

'The Peace Corps? She wants to join the Peace Corps this summer. That doesn't seem right.'

We had recently decided to send Wendy to a work camp the following summer. She had heartily disliked the idea. The night before, Wendy, my wife and I were discussing the matter. My wife said, 'It's a sort of junior Peace Corps.' Wendy immediately grasped the concept, became quite excited at the idea and began to look forward to going to the work camp. The discussion had not been mentioned to anyone else by my wife, my daughter, or myself.

At this point Mrs Garrett stopped talking. I waited a moment, took the first box back and slid the second one – the tuft of hair from the dog – beneath her fingers.

Mrs Garrett's Comments
Box 2
'Oh, he's a nice dog. I'd like to take him hunting. He gets a lot of burrs in his coat. I think he once had a very bad pain in his paw. It really hurt him badly, didn't it?'

Discussion

He does often get burrs in his coat, but so do most dogs in the suburbs and country, I imagine. I answered this by saying, 'I don't know. The neighbours just moved in.' That evening I asked the neighbours if the dog had ever had any trouble with a paw. They answered that the previous year he had cut a forepaw on a piece of glass in the garden of their home. It had become badly infected and they had expected it to be fatal. He spent six weeks at the veterinary hospital.

'Tell me, didn't he once have a Sealyham companion?'

I replied again that I did not know. (Further I did not add, but it was true, that knowing nothing about dogs, I would not have known a Sealyham if one came up and bit me.) That evening when I asked our neighbour about this he replied, 'I thought you didn't know anything about dogs. He's a purebred Welsh terrier with Kennel Club papers to prove it, but there is something about his bone structure so that every time we show him to a real dog fancier, he says, "Oh, come now, there's a little Sealyham in him somewhere."'

Mrs Garrett again stopped speaking and I took the second box and slid the third (the rosebud) under her fingers.

Mrs Garrett's Comments
Box 3
'It's the rosebud. It comes from a very small garden. The garden needs a lot of work before it's ready for the summer.'

Discussion

These statements are true but could have been intuitively guessed by anyone who had formed a fairly accurate picture of my personality. Knowing that I lived in a suburb, it would be a reasonable guess that I took it from my own garden. Knowing me, it would also be a reasonable guess that if I had a garden it would be a small one and that it would very likely to be neglected and need a lot of work to be ready for the summer.

'The soil is too acid for it to grow well.'

I had been told this several times by people who knew something about gardening. However, it is entirely possible that someone raised in the country – as Mrs Garrett was – could have known this from looking at the rosebud. Further, this soil condition is very common – almost universal – in the area in which I lived.

In this 'spontaneous' psychometry experiment, all the statements made were accurate. Some were extremely precise – as the 'American History' statement. Some – as the statements about the dog's paw and the 'Sealyham companion' – were unknown to anyone present and presumably to anyone Mrs Garrett had ever met. Interestingly enough, the statement about the 'Sealyham companion' and the statements of dog fanciers that '. . . there's a little Sealyham in him somewhere' (referring to his bone structure) appears to illustrate the typical clairvoyant problem of finding it difficult to differentiate realistic and symbolic levels of perception and description.

The facts that the decision to bring new materials to the experiment was made after seeing Mrs Garrett, and in her absence; that the materials were chosen pretty much at random, and that no one was told of this until they were handed to her increase the impressiveness of this 'spontaneous experiment'. It should be emphasized perhaps that the procedure we were working on at the time was dermal vision and not psychometry, and that her statements were 'off-the-cuff' and spontaneous.

9

DO WE SURVIVE DEATH ?

The philosophy of the day must concern itself with the actual facts of the day's experience, or it becomes irrelevant and useless. There is little point in trying to formulate 'the principles of mind and body' and then to relate the present 'wonder' about the mind to the answer to that old question. The philosophers must now reckon with the evidence and experiments of today and find their position accordingly.[1]

We are now faced with a curious, unexpected, and not very welcome problem, and must look at it and at its implications.

The problem is this: from the viewpoint of the research programme just described, it is not possible to differentiate Type B perception of information from the living from Type B perception of information from the dead. Procedures that examine psi-occurrences and their relations to the maintenance of our roles, relationships, identity, etc., do not differentiate on the basis of whether or not the other individuals involved are now biologically alive. Type B perceptions generally do not make this differentiation.

Although this conclusion was reached in the evaluation of a proposed research programme, others have reached it before. Gardner Murphy, in his study of the results of mediumship, wrote:

> [In certain cases, the only way the medium could have obtained the information] would be a telepathic interchange with some other source possessing the facts. The dynamics, however, of such interchange would probably be the same whether the source of the information is incarnate or discarnate, alive or deceased.[2]

149

This relates to something pointed out in Chapter 6. This is the fact that Type B perceptions (ESP occurrences) are influenced far more (at least) by the *history* the other person involved (or the 'target' in clairvoyance) has with us than by the *properties* of the other person or the target. Just as being located at a particular place is a property of the other person, so is being biologically alive or dead.[3]

As startling a fact as this – that our research procedure does not differentiate between communicating with the living or the dead – must have implications. What are some of them? The first one that comes to mind is: if Type B perceptions, consisting, as we have seen, of events in the Realm of Consciousness, cannot differentiate on the basis of an individual having died or not, do we observe biological death in this realm?

The answer to the question, as stated, is, of course, 'No.' We do not observe *any* biological occurrences in this realm. We must restate the question. We could, perhaps, ask: 'Do we observe a total and complete cessation of consciousness at the moment of biological death?' The answer again is, perforce, 'No.' We can never observe another person's consciousness, and have no experience with our own biological death.

What question *can* we ask? We shall have to go far to find the answer. We shall have to approach it in a roundabout way (which, as the White Queen taught Alice, is sometimes the only way to get there).

We should not be too surprised that we are involved with the question of conscious survival of bodily death. First, we have noted the fact that entities, guiding principles and observables in some realms – even those of the stature of 'space', 'time', 'purpose', 'specific-event-causation', 'temperature', 'shape' and 'size' – exist in these realms and do not exist (or have an entirely different meaning) in others. There are vast differences between what exists and how things happen in different realms. In the Realm of the Very-Large-and-Fast, where the relevant geometry is Riemannian rather than Euclidean, parallel lines do meet, the shortest distance between two points is not a straight line, and space is infinite, but has a finite diameter. What is utterly unthinkable in one realm is commonplace in another.

Secondly, it was this question ('survival') that led to the study of large scale psi-occurrences in the early days of psychical research.

As we return to the study of these events, it seems reasonable that we should again find ourselves facing our original problem.

It may well be that the problem of 'survival' belongs to a special class of problems first defined by the philosopher Immanuel Kant. He said that there was a group of questions that human beings must confront, but which are rationally undecidable. In this class, in which we can logically prove both negative and positive answers, he included the existence of God and the freedom of the will. If survival belongs in this class of problems, we must at least face the fact that the subject is logically open. But perhaps with the aid of new concepts, concepts that Kant did not have, we can go further.

It is certainly and unquestionably true that biological death is an observable in the sensory realm. 'All men are mortal,' is the sad truth long known to all of us. Whoever disputes it is a madman. Our question, however, is a different one: Do we observe death in the Realm of Consciousness, and, if not, what – if any – are the implications of this?

The body exists – is observed in – the sensory realm. Each body eventually dies. All cultures we have known of agree on this, although they have often disagreed on *why* all bodies die. Some cultures feel it is always due to hostile and malign attacks; some that it only dies when medicine or prayer fail; some that it simply wears out and that this is part of the natural order. Other explanations exist.

Consciousness exists in a different realm than the physical body, and there has been vast and complete disagreement among different cultures as to whether it continues to exist when the body dies, and – if not – what happens to it. In itself, this disagreement emphasises the complexity and difficulty of the problem.

Further, we can easily (if not comfortably) intellectually grasp the death of the body; the non-existence of our own consciousness, or that of someone close to us, is not comprehensible. Our minds become giddy as we try to comprehend it. The idea slips out of our grasp. Freud once remarked that no man could comprehend the idea of his own death and non-existence. This is true also of those others who have convinced us of the existence of their consciousness through strong personal interaction. The idea of our, or their, consciousness no longer existing is so incomprehensible that we generally prefer to think of other things.

Indeed, if modern brain physiologists of the stature of

Sherrington and Penfield are correct, and if the metaphor that the brain is an organ producing and secreting thought as the liver does bile is outworn and no longer fits the data of brain anatomy and physiology, then certain implications follow. One is that we can no longer depend on the authority of 'science' for the belief that consciousness ceases to exist with the death of the body. (Whether we ever had the right to depend on it in this way is certainly open to argument, but many of us felt that we could.) The analogy with the new view that comes most easily to mind is that if my television set is an instrument of liaison between myself and a television station, and my set is destroyed, I have no reason to suppose that the station has gone out of existence, although the communication has been lost. As far as communication with me is concerned, Walter Cronkite no longer exists. However, Mr Cronkite might well dispute the idea that this means that he is dead.

As I have attempted to demonstrate in this book, entities and observables existing in one realm of experience may not exist in others. Different kinds of explanation, different but compatible metaphysical systems, must be used in different realms if we are to make our data coherent and meaningful. What are we to make of the fact that death is not observed in the Realm of Consciousness?

First, we must rid ourselves of some preconceptions we may be bringing to the problem. For example, that we can apply 'common sense' to it. Common sense has been defined by the philosopher Suzanne Langer as 'the accepted metaphysics of your generation'. Nevertheless it is an essential and invaluable guide to the sensory realm. Whether you are a modern American and observe that your automobile tyres are thin and must be replaced before you take a long trip to the mountains, or whether you are a Trobriand Islander and observe that your canoe paddles are splintered and worn and need to be replaced before you take a long trip to the next island, common sense is essential agreement as to how to behave in the sensory realm. *In this realm, where the entities and observables can be seen and touched, common sense works. In other realms it does not.* We cannot solve the problems of the Realm of the Very Small with the common sense derived from our experience with the sensory realm. Nor problems in the Realm of Consciousness.

What is plain as a pikestaff in one realm of experience may not exist in another. A human being's meaningful behaviour has 'purpose', a molecule's movements do not. A tree has shape, an electron does not. A bar of iron moving at a few hundred miles an hour relative to me has a position and movement in space that can be described separately from its position and movement in time. The same bar of iron moving at close to the speed of light relative to me can not. Our bar of iron has a temperature, the molecules of which it is made up do not. My skull is located in space, my consciousness is not. My brain cells have a size, my fear has not.

A flashlight is pointed up into the sky and turned on. After a few moments we turn the flashlight off and then take a hammer and destroy it. The beam of light continues to travel through space. Even if we hold a full funeral for the flashlight and bury it in hallowed ground, the beam of light goes on. What we have done is to take some objects in the sensory realm – batteries, wires, an electric bulb, a switch – put them together in a particular way, and produced an entity in a different realm, an entity that did not exist before.

Our two entities – the flashlight and the beam of light – turn out to be in different realms, and to have very different fates. The second survives the destruction of the first.

Therefore, when we say that the body has death inevitably awaiting it, and ask if this is also true of consciousness, which exists in a different realm of experience, the question is not as simple-minded as it may appear at first.

There is public access to the body. It exists in the sensory realm, and we can observe the body of another person as it moves and breathes and maintains itself, and as it ceases to do these things. There is only private access to consciousness, and we can never observe the consciousness of another person either before or after the biological death of the body. What we *observe* is the death of the body. What we *infer* is the death of consciousness. These are two separate constructs yet we treat them as one. It would be equally valid, to return to our analogy of the flashlight, to say that the beam of light is also destroyed. We can no longer observe it. We have no contact with it. Scientifically, however, we have good reason to know it continues to exist.

Many of us, however, feel a conviction that consciousness dies with the body. We say, 'Oh, if we could only believe in survival! How much easier and better it would make our lives.'

This statement is actually far from the truth for a great many of us. How many of us would really want the *responsibility* for our lives and behaviour that would follow if we really were certain of survival with its – to us – implied probability of trial and of punishment and reward? Which of us would face with equanimity the possibility of a just God and a just trial?

Further, a belief in survival would make us give up the simplest theory about how-the-world-works that we humans have ever devised. Naïve materialism and mechanism are the simplest and least thought-provoking theories about how things are that we have ever devised, which is one reason why we hang on to them so strongly in the teeth of so much contrary evidence.

All our experience and training in evaluating what is going on in another person's consciousness is derived from activity in the sensory realm. We observe what their body is doing and extra-polate to their consciousness. It is the only way we have. We know that we may be wrong. A person may pretend to be sad when they are not. Or vice versa, as in the 'laugh, clown, laugh' concept. A person may even pretend to be unconscious when they are not. However, this is the way we must operate. We therefore auto-matically come to the conclusion that when the body ceases to be active, consciousness no longer exists. Although we have a large amount of evidence that this may not be so – as in surgical anaesthesia situations or in severe catatonia, where the person afterwards displays an awareness of, or reaction to, what went on when they were apparently unconscious – we still hold to the established belief. This is so strong that a potential major medical procedure of great value has not been put into action. Several experiments have shown conclusively that positive suggestion given to patients who have just undergone surgery under anaesthesia and are still 'unconscious' in the recovery room produces very definite positive results – such as rapidity of healing, the reduction of negative side effects, less need for pain killers during recovery, a more rapid recovery period and so on.

This evidence is now so clear that if it were an available drug that produced these results, instead of a verbal communication, any hospital that did not use it routinely would be regarded as being badly behind the times. These experiments have been completely ignored by the medical profession because of the assumptions we make about the identical course followed by the body and con-sciousness. It takes a very strong counter-belief – as in strong religious convictions – to change this assumption.[4]

We feel – from an unverbalized acceptance of the concept that everything in the cosmos works, and can be explained, in the same way – that we have daily proof of the idea that consciousness dies with the body. We see machines ceasing to function and sent to the scrap pile, in very much the same way that we see bodies ceasing to function and being irretrievably destroyed. No consciousness is left of the machines, nothing is left but a memory, or, in some cases, its productions – the thread from a thread-making machine, children, or the books left behind by a writer. Since we assume that everything in the world works in the same way, we assume that machines and humans end in the same final and complete manner. We forget that this is a hypothesis and very far from an established truth.

One of the things we forget in using the machine model for living organisms is that there are great differences between these two classes of entities. As only one example, a machine can be taken apart into its basic components and reassembled so that it will then work as well as before. In spite of the legend of the success of Dr Frankenstein, this cannot be done with living organisms.

Since our society has, by and large, accepted the belief that consciousness dies with the body as a 'truth', let us look for a moment at the meaning of this term. What do we mean by 'truth' today?

The term has, it turns out, three meanings. A truth can be empirical, analytic or scientific. An *empirical truth* is one given by direct observation. In a vacuum all bodies fall with constant acceleration. I have just been outside and seen and felt that it was raining. I have had a direct experience of God.

We have no empirical truth concerning the death of consciousness. We can only observe a breakdown of communication. These are quite different things, as our analogy with the television set and Walter Cronkite makes plain.

An *analytic truth* is one that analysis of the parts of the statement makes inexorable. I analyze the meaning of the terms in the statement '2 times 2 = 4'. The truth of the statement is plain in the meaning of '2' and 'times' and '=' and '4'. Or I define God as a perfect being. Perfection includes existence. Therefore, God exists. The truth of the logical syllogism is analytic truth.

We have no analytic truth concerning the death of consciousness. There is nothing in the definition of consciousness, nor in a scientific definition of the relationship of mind and body, that inexorably leads to the truth that when the body dies, consciousness ceases.

A *scientific truth* is one that is triply anchored. It rests both on empirical observation and on formal analysis, like the analyses of pure mathematics. Further, it has testable implications – it has 'logical fertility'. If I say empirically, 'I have had a direct experience of God and observed that He is real and good and omnipotent and that He will therefore respond to intercessory prayer', I know analytically that He exists because the world exists, and whatever exists must be created; therefore, there is a Creator. I then make a series of tests and find that intercessory prayer gets results. I now have a scientific truth (which, like any other truth, is open to revision with new observations, analyses and experiments).

Newton's laws obtained the status of scientific truths as they were empirically anchored in the exact observations of Tycho Brahe, analytically anchored in Kepler's laws as well as their own logical coherence, and predicted accurately a host of phenomena – solar positions, tide movements, falling fruit and other objects, and so forth.

We have no scientific truth concerning the annihilation of consciousness at the death of the body.

It might be said that all this arises from the fact that there is only private access in consciousness – that only I can observe my consciousness and only you can observe yours. This is, in large part, true, but does not change things at all. Much of the strange goings on in the quantum realm could be, as truly, said to arise from the fact that the entities and observables involved are much too small to see or touch, even theoretically. This is true, but does not change the strangeness (from the viewpoint of the sensory realm and 'common sense') of what is going on. We are dealing with different *realms of experience,* not of different realms of existence. 'Realms of existence' is, from the viewpoint of modern science, a meaningless term. It is our experience and possibility of experience (as in 'thought experiments') that, alloyed with whatever is 'out there', shapes scientific truth as well as other kinds of truth.

'Death' is a construct, a system we organize in order to relate a group of observables. To make the matter clearer, let us examine the construct of a 'star'. We observe a point of light. It has observables – brightness, position, size, direction, perhaps periodicity. We measure these and presently add heat and distance. We organize the 'system' or 'construct' of a star. It *possesses* or *carries* these observables.

The observables that death carries are cessation of movement, loss of communication, failure of self-maintenance (unopposed action of the second law of thermodynamics). Nowhere is there an observable in the Realm of Consciousness. The construct of death is a well-organized one of the sensory realm. And only of this realm.

We are not talking here about the *existence* of consciousness. That is a matter beyond rational dispute. We are talking about the *cessation* of this existence, which is an entirely different matter ('construct', 'system'). To make the problem clearer: I have a pair of shoes in the closet. I know they are there empirically – I see and touch them any time I wish to. I know they are there rationally – I remember buying them and putting them there; I am a person who wears shoes in this climate; shoes are widely worn by human beings for practical reasons I can name, etc.; I can make predictions that, since the closet is locked and I have the only key, they will be there when I go to look for them; when I wear them, my feet will be warmer and dryer than when I do not, etc. Thus, that they are there is also a scientific truth. The *disappearance* of the shoes, their ceasing to exist, is quite a separate phenomenon. I may lose the key and not be able to open the closet door, but I have no reason, empirically, rationally or scientifically, to suppose that they have ceased to exist.

The example is trivial. Nevertheless, it may illustrate the difference between the existence of consciousness and its annihilation at bodily death.

What we have been saying so far in this chapter is that there is – from the viewpoint of modern science – no reason to believe that consciousness stops with the biological death of the body. At the very least, the question is wide open. Do we have anything to say from this viewpoint in the other direction?

It is a basic rule of science, a rule developed over a long period of work, that if an entity, a construct, is not observable, then science treats the entity as non-existent. This, we have found, is by far the most fruitful course to follow. It grew out of the principle of parsimony, which says that it is unwise to multiply entities unnecessarily, and out of our experience in exploring scientific constructs and concepts.

When the experiments by Michelson and Morley demonstrated that the 'ether' (a universal substance filling the cosmos, whose existence was widely believed in at that time) could not be observed, nor could its effects be observed, it was decided that science would henceforth treat the ether as non-existent. This was so widely accepted that most physics textbooks reported that these experiments had proved the ether did not exist. What they had actually demonstrated is that it could not be observed. Further, the fact that it existed or did not exist produced no consequences. There were no differences in what we could observe if there actually was an ether or if there was not.

Consciousness is a construct whose existence has certainly achieved the status of a scientific truth. It is a primary observation, an empirical and analytic truth that has consequences. (I can predict that when I wake up tomorrow morning, I will perceive my consciousness as belonging to me and not to someone else. Or, when I have a pain, it will be in my leg and not in yours. If I know someone very well and have a 'feel' of their consciousness and how it operates, I can make a pretty good guess as to how they will behave in many circumstances.)

The annihilation of consciousness is something else entirely. It is not an empirical nor an analytic truth. It cannot be observed. I cannot observe mine. Because of the private access to consciousness, I cannot observe anyone else's either. There is nothing in the definition of body or consciousness that leads us analytically to be clear that the death of the body must lead to the death of the mind.

Further, the existence of the construct of annihilation of consciousness does not have consequences in anything which we can observe. The death of another person's body results in the loss of our ability to communicate with them and to experience their consciousness. *Whether or not their consciousness is annihilated, the result is the same.* They can only express the existence of their consciousness through their body. When it dies, this ability disappears. The result is the same whether or not their consciousness continues to exist. When my television set is destroyed, whether nor or not the television station is also destroyed is without observable consequences.

Therefore, the concept of the annihilation of the consciousness at the death of the body is an idea with no consequences that we can observe. If we wish to be consistent methodologically, we must say that the concept of the annihilation of consciousness at bodily death is very similar to the concept of the ether, and must be treated in the same way: as non-existent. We thus come to the conclusion that, from a scientific viewpoint, consciousness continues after the death of the body.

The intention of this chapter has not been to convince readers of 'survival', of the continued existence of consciousness after bodily death. No intellectual argument is going to convince anyone of an answer to this question. It simply is not the sort of question that can be meaningfully answered in this way.

The purpose of this chapter, rather, has been to dispel the myth that a scientific approach to this question leads inexorably to the answer that consciousness is annihilated at bodily death. As we have seen, an approach following the strict methodology of twentieth-century science leads to the opposite conclusion.

The problem of survival in psychical research will have to be approached and answered in terms of the data of psychical research, not in terms of a preconceived belief as to what a scientific answer must be.

10
CONSCIOUSNESS AND THE ORGANIZATION OF REALITY

In all investigations, the answers you get depend on the questions you ask: the questions you ask depend on the assumptions you make and the assumptions you make depend on how much you think you know, even more on how much you take for granted, and most of all, in serious investigation, on how willing you are to accept what William James called the pain of a new idea. [1]

Renee Haynes

There is one other aspect of the Realm of Consciousness that it is important to present here. The importance of this aspect for psychical research was brought home to me during the research on psychic healing that is reported in Chapter 11.

I have pointed out the obvious fact that consciousness observes the outside world and then largely disappears into this perception. It is, in Fry's words, 'a glass and a transparency'. Our usual concern is with the 'outside' world we perceive, not with our consciousness. Even when our feelings are overwhelmingly strong, such as at a time of extreme depression, we continue this focus. We say that 'Everything is hopeless, the world is terrible', rather than 'My consciousness has a strongly depressed tone today and casts a blackness over everything I perceive.'

We are concerned primarily with the outside world (including, of course, our own bodies), but it is a world that we do not just perceive: it is a world that we organize into coherent and consistent patterns. We choose an organizing pattern and then organize our sensations with it. At this point in the modern development of scientific knowledge, we are clear that the world we perceive is at least as much our invention as it is our discovery.[2]

This is not the place to go into this point in detail. It has been done so well in books such as Abel's *Man is the Measure*[3] that it should not be repeated here. In addition, I have devoted an entire book to this in the past,[4] and it is covered extensively in a recent book by Henry Margenau and myself.[5]

Nevertheless, it is important here to stress that we use definite organizing systems to put the sensed world together into the perceived world. Without the organizing powers of consciousness, the universe would be, in Einstein's words, 'a mere rubbish heap'. In his usual succinct style, Bertrand Russell put it: 'Order, unity and continuity are human inventions just as truly as catalogues and encyclopaedias.'

Our consciousness organizes the world according to a specific plan, and changes this plan from time to time. Although there are a very large variety of organizational plans, they tend to fall into four general classes. These four classes of ways of organizing reality so that it is coherent and can be efficiently dealt with might be illustrated by the following account of a day in the life of a particular businessman.

In this man's everyday work, as he sits at his desk, he lives in a reality we all know very well. It's the reality we think of ordinarily in the West as the real one. It is the reality in which we tie our shoelaces and design the shoes, in which we buy airplane tickets and take a taxi to the airport. The businessman would say, as would most of us, that this is the only *real* reality and every other one is due to some aberration or other, usually temporary.

One day the businessman comes home after work. He knows there has been some meningitis in the area and he's worried about his three-year-old child. Sitting downstairs in the evening, he hears the child crying upstairs. As he goes upstairs he is terribly frightened. He finds himself pleading: 'Please, don't let it be meningitis.' He is really praying. His whole consciousness is involved in this action. He is completely organized in such a way that this is the only thing that makes sense to him and that what he is doing at that point is the most reasonable action he could undertake. He does not question it. At that moment he is perceiving and reacting to a different reality from normal because when he is at work, there is absolutely no point in such pleading. The universe, as he ordinarily construes it, does not respond to emotion and prayer.

He arrives upstairs and finds to his vast relief that the child is not ill. The child has awakened in the night upset and frightened. He soothes the child. He holds the child in his arms and says, 'It's all right.' What is really happening here? The child has awakened confused and frightened, and the businessman reassures him by saying, 'It's all right. The universe is friendly. Things are all right.' Now in his ordinary, everyday state of consciousness, the way he ordinarily organizes reality, this is certainly not true.

He lives in a world that eventually will kill both the businessman and the child and annihilate them both. One cannot say this to a child and also say 'It's all right, the universe is friendly'. But the businessman is not lying. At this moment he is in a completely different reality than he was during the day or when he was coming up the stairs. Out of a deep sincerity he is saying, in effect: There is a way of being in the universe where love transcends death and where the cosmos will not annihilate us. Again, he has organized reality in a different way. And this is the way, at this moment, he perceives, reacts to, reality; this is what he *knows* at this moment to be the complete truth.[6]

After reassuring the child, the businessman comes downstairs. That evening he and his wife go dancing. During the evening he is dancing in his usual way, enjoying it more or less, thinking of various things, the music, his partner, what they'd been talking about, other people, and so forth. Suddenly he realizes that for a period of time, he is not sure exactly how long, everything was different. During this period of time he was not thinking about anything. He was not in a daze. He was not in a trance. He was not asleep. As a matter of fact, he was very wide awake and alert, but his whole being was doing just one thing: dancing. After it was over he felt good, 'charged up', slightly 'high', and very pleasantly relaxed. During the period that had passed, if it is analyzed carefully, we find that again he had organized reality in a different way. He was no longer listening *to* the music, dancing *with* his wife, *avoiding* the other people, etc.; rather, he and the music and his partner were, in a very fundamental sense, one. He was moving as if he were part of a network that included the music, the floor, the other people, and so forth. Thinking, feeling and doing were one and the same thing. He was dancing far better than he ordinarily did. It was almost as if he and his wife had a kind of telepathy between them, and responded to each other's movements and to each other's perceptions in a way far superior to the ordinary way. In the reality he was living at that moment, there were no separations between things. All things flowed into each other.

Later that evening, at home, he and his wife sit listening to a Beethoven Sonata. During many portions of the music he again organizes the universe in a different way than he does in his ordinary, everyday work at his desk. He organizes it in such a way that it is not he who is listening to the music; the music and he again are one. The music is inside as much as it is outside. He is not talking about it. He is not thinking about it, but just intensely *being* with the music.

That night, he goes to sleep and during his sleep he has a dream. In the dream strange things happen. A kangaroo appears and hops around a mountain. Somehow it has the face of his older brother. He talks to it. The scene shifts and is now underwater. A beautiful mermaid sings. During the dream he does not question the 'strange' things that happen. He knows they are right. He has organized reality again in a different way, in a way in which all things are possible, all connections can be made, the symbol and the thing it symbolizes interact with each other constantly. This again is another state of consciousness, another reality in which our subject lives.

One of the fascinating things about alternate realities is that, at the time you are really using one, it makes perfect sense to you and you know it is the only correct way to view reality. It is only common sense.

In the modern phrase, the businessman was in an altered state of consciousness in each of these different incidents. Each of us, every day, uses several different constructions of the universe. We are in 'altered states of consciousness', we are using 'different constructions of reality', we are using 'different metaphysical systems', we are in 'alternate realities'. All the evidence we have is that this is essential to us. Certainly it is universal; it occurs in every culture and in every age we know of. If we encourage the use of alternate realities, as in meditation, play, serious music, and so forth, we increase the ability of human beings to reach toward new potentials.

The social scientist deals with the problem of alternate realities by asking how the individual (or the culture the social scientist is studying) is construing the world at a particular time or in a particular situation. This is to ask: what is the set of rules that are seen to be operating in the total cosmos — everything 'that is' — by his subjects. In the experience of the social scientist, people tend to use one construction of reality at a time and to change these fluidly and easily, very often without noticing that there has been a change. As the experienced European traveller changes his language easily as he crosses borders, so do we change the systems by means of which we organize reality.

When a person is dreaming he invests the whole of reality with the laws that govern the dream. When he is trying to cross a busy road h́e invests the whole of reality with an entirely different set of laws. As we have shown in the case of our apocryphal businessman, this set of observables and laws, seen as operating in all reality, changes a number of times a day for all of us.

As indicated elsewhere, these different ways of construing and perceiving the world are not only ways of increasing the potential of human beings; they are necessary for their fullest humanhood. There is a large and growing body of evidence that suggests a need for humans to be-in-the-world in each of these four general ways. Indeed, it is beginning to seem more and more reasonable that much of our social (and personal) pathology may be related to a lack of ability to express these needs for being. Repressing a part of themselves, that part which needs to express itself through a particular mode of organizing reality, many people pay the inevitable price for rejecting a part of what it means to be human. The price is paid in anger against the self and against others. Plutarch wrote:

> If we traverse the world, it is possible to find cities without walls, without letters, without wealth, without coin, without schools or theatres; but a city without a temple, or that practices not worship, prayers, and the like, no one has ever seen.

Today we would add that no one ever saw a city where the inhabitants did not play, dream, deal effectively with objects according to the rules of the see-touch realm, or have ways of organizing reality so that there are no boundaries within it and everything is a dynamic One.

The four classes of ways of organizing reality that we tend today to see as universal and also as necessary for an individual to achieve his fullest potential are as follows:

1. *The Sensory Reality.* This is the everyday 'common-sense' Western way of organizing reality. It is the way that our businessman used when he was at his desk and working. It is what the mystics tend to call 'The Way of the Many'. We all know the laws and basic limiting principles of this organization of reality very well. It is essential to biological survival and is the way that must be used to cross a busy road and not be run over. Its laws and entities are very similar to those of the see-touch Realm of Experience.

2. *The Clairvoyant or Unity Reality.* This is the way of organizing reality that the businessman used when he was dancing, and later when he was listening to Beethoven. In this way of organizing reality there are no boundaries and nothing is separate from anything else. All things flow into each other and are part of a larger whole that makes up the entire cosmos. The individual relates to the whole as the single brushstroke relates to the entire painting or the single note to the symphony of which it is a part. The mystics have tended to call this 'The Way of the One'.

3. *The Transpsychic Reality.* This is the way of organizing reality that the businessman was using when he was praying, 'Please don't let it be meningitis.' In this construction of 'what is', the individual is perceived as an entity that exists in its own right, but it is also a part of the total One of the cosmos so that no definite line of separation is possible. The analogy of the wave and the ocean is often used. Similarly, we see references to the fingers and the hand, or to the arm and the body, in the descriptions of this reality. It is the construction of reality in which intercessory prayer is perceived as effective. The individual is seen as separate enough to have wishes and desires, but connected enough so that it is possible to 'urge' these on the great forces that make up the total cosmos.

4. *The Mythic Reality.* It was this construction of reality that the businessman was using when he was dreaming. It is the way reality is organized in play, myth and sympathetic magic. In this way of organizing reality, anything can be identical with anything else once they have been connected with each other – spatially, temporally or conceptually. The part is identical with the whole,

the name with the thing, and the symbol with its object. Each can be treated as if it were the other. The world is full of all kinds of possible combinations and syntheses. The relationship between this reality, play and creativity has been remarked upon by a number of observers. This mode is necessary to keep us fresh and alive, curious and creative. Without it, 'All work and no play makes Jack a dull boy', as the old saying goes, and there is truth in it. Without the ability to use this mode of being, we become bored, and the sunset, our daily life, and even sexual activity become dull affairs.

I am aware that this has been a very brief statement of the ways of organizing reality, but I hesitate to repeat what we have described in greater length elsewhere.[4,5]

Two further things, however, must be said here about the different 'realities' I have listed. First, I have described them as metaphysical systems with their own laws and definitions. This is a valid approach and the only way to describe them clearly. However, from the experiential point of view, they are states of consciousness. When the individual is perceiving the world and reacting to it as if one set of basic limiting principles is the *real* one, he is in an 'altered' state of consciousness – altered from the everyday waking Western state of consciousness.

Second, these various states of consciousness deal with the same phenomena, but with different conceptions of how reality works and the nature of its laws and goals – different definitions of space, time, causality, how things interact, and what is the nature of a 'thing'. But it is the same phenomena. Whatever it is, we take from whatever is 'there', we carve up in different ways, as Monet, Leger, Picasso and Wyeth will each find a different painting in the same model.

To sum up, the social scientist has become aware that his subjects – individuals and cultures – use a number of different conceptions of reality at different times. He has studied these and analyzed the rules and laws used in them, and under what conditions each is used. His basic attitude, with a few exceptions, has been that there is only one 'correct' conception of reality, the Western, waking, 'common-sense' description of reality. This is essentially the descriptive picture which the physicist applies to the sensory realm, the see-touch realm, and generally corresponds to what is usually called 'classical' physics.

Due to this belief in the correctness of this description of reality and the general belief in our culture that the entire universe is run on the same principles, the social scientist has usually attempted to deal with the data in his field of research as if they fitted the see-touch picture of reality. Stating this in another way, the social scientist decided in advance of gathering and interpreting his data what basic laws and what kind of laws would make it coherent and lawful.

This is apparently one of the reasons for the tremendous problems that exist today in the social sciences, and for the general lack of progress made in many parts of these fields of study. Major progress was made in physics in many areas only when the machine model was abandoned as a system of explanation – a description of reality – in these areas. When this was carried further, and it was realized that the general description of reality used in the sensory realm was inapplicable for dealing with many different kinds of data, even greater progress resulted.

I am saying here that much greater progress would be made in parapsychology and in the social sciences generally when its practitioners abandon the assumption that there is only one set of principles on which the entire cosmos operates, and that this can be most accurately represented by the principles and laws of the see-touch realm, essentially the machine model of reality.

The Realm of Consciousness is the only realm known at present in which the entire organizing scheme by means of which data from it become coherent changes from time to time. Therefore, we have a new question to ask about Type B perceptions. We have asked in what realms of experience they were observed, and found that they were observed in two realms: the Realm of Consciousness and the Realm of Meaningful Behaviour. We must now ask, 'When we observe Type B perceptions in the Realm of Consciousness, are they related to a particular mode of organizing reality? If so, does this help us to understand the phenomenon any further?'

The next chapter, on psychic healing, will develop these questions further in the exploration of a particular type of psi-occurrence.

11
A RESEARCH PROJECT IN PSYCHIC HEALING

One of the major points that this book has been making is that there is nothing 'paranormal' or paradoxical about those types of perception studied by psychical research. Indeed, they are no more mysterious than (or they are just as mysterious as) the processes and activities studied by university and college psychology departments.

A counter to this claim might run as follows: 'What you say may be true for Type B perceptions, what we call telepathy, clairvoyance or precognition. But what about psychic healing? Here is a phenomenon in which the healer does mental gymnastics in his own head, or else waves his hands in esoteric passes over the patient's body. Sometimes the patient, perhaps at a considerable distance from the healer, perhaps not even knowing the procedure is being carried out, shows medically unexpected, biological improvement. Surely, one cannot claim that this is not a "paranormal" phenomenon in every sense of the word?'

This certainly seems to be a valid point. Further, if one asks healers exactly what they are doing, they will usually speak of 'sending energy to the patient', 'channelling God's love to the patient', 'focusing etheric energy on the damaged area', or other exotic explanations of the same type. There seems to be little doubt that the healers themselves believe they are performing 'paranormal' activities. If they are correct, the whole approach of this book collapses. It would be very hard to see how we could carry out a scientific study of the process of 'channelling God's love to the patient', beyond making an attempt to assess the personality characteristics of the healers in order to determine what standards God uses to choose 'channels'. Or we might try to determine the limitations of the Almighty by making lists of the kinds of diseases that healers were successful with and those that they were not. Both of these approaches would smack of *hubris,* not to say *chutzpah.*

However, it is important to note that what people believe and say they are doing is often a far cry from what they actually *are* doing. The fact that an eighteenth-century scientist, successfully lighting a fire in his grate, believed that he was burning the 'caloric fluid' in the wood does not mean that there was any caloric fluid to burn. It will be necessary to look much closer at the activities of psychic healers before we accept the fact that their sincere explanations have any more relationship to the facts of the matter than did those of Renaissance physicians who bled their patients in order to remove excess humours.

That, in many areas at least, psychic healers are not the best judges of what constitutes their activities can be demonstrated scientifically. A recent study by Shirley Winston (herself both a professional scientist and an accomplished psychic healer) investigated the question of how well a healer should know or be acquainted with those who sought their help in order to get the best results. Dr Winston asked a number of healers if they would get the best results if they knew the subject well, knew him superficially, had only a letter and a photograph of him, or only had a lock of the subject's hair. All the healers had strong opinions about the conditions under which they would expect to obtain the best results. Experiment demonstrated, however, that in nearly every case these opinions were wrong.[1]

It is also true that nearly all healers believe very strongly that they obtain the best results when they are calm, relaxed, and under as little tension from the outside press of events as possible. Again, experimental evidence does not show this to be true.[2]

If we cannot rely on what healers *say* about their work, we must examine what they actually *do.* An examination – in person or through their writing – of a large number of apparently serious and dedicated psychic healers revealed two types of activity. The first consisted of idiosyncratic behaviours – behaviours performed by individual healers only or by healers having a specific training or cultural background. These behaviours included chanting, praying, washing the hands, aligning themselves with the magnetic lines of the earth, invoking various deities and agencies, establishing 'rapport' with various types of non-human beings, and so forth.

The second group consisted of those behaviours performed by *all* the healers studied – *universal* behaviours. Only one such behaviour was found in the group. At some point during the process they defined as 'the healing encounter', the healers all altered their mode of consciousness. They changed the plan by means of which they structured and organized reality. They changed from the Sensory Mode to the Unitary or Clairvoyant Mode (see Chapter 10), with the person they were healing as the focus.

I assumed that the only universal behaviour I found among my group of evaluated healers was the crucial factor that (insofar as this factor came from the healers) contributed the positive results observed in the field of psychic healing.[3] I therefore trained myself to move into the Unitary state of consciousness with the healee, as I shall call the person requiring healing, as the focus. Rather to my astonishment, I found that the results I now obtained included occasional positive biological changes that did not seem attributable to suggestion or to a placebo effect. In short, I, who had never had a psychic experience in my life, had now become a reasonably competent psychic healer.

A typical incident was the following. A married couple – close friends of mine – lived in California, across the continent from me. I had not communicated with them for several months. The man, on a business trip to Chicago, called me on the telephone to chat. During the talk, he mentioned that his wife, who had been under rather heavy emotional stress for some time, had such severe arthritis of the right shoulder that for a few months she had not been able to raise her right arm above the neck level and, indeed, could not move it at all without pain ranging from moderate to severe. A variety of medical treatments had not improved the situation, and they were at a loss as to what to do next.

I suggested that it could do no harm to try a psychic healing and (knowing her well enough to be sure that she would welcome the idea if asked) further said that I would prefer to try for a time without her being told. In this way, the possibility of suggestion would be much less.

That night I got myself relaxed and 'centred' and shifted my consciousness so that I was construing the world in the Unitary Mode, with the woman as a focus. I perceived her as part of the total One of the cosmos, of which I also, and everything else in my consciousness, was a part. All things, she and myself included, flowed into one another as part of the 'seamless garment' that made up reality. I achieved this state of consciousness several times for what seemed like ten or fifteen seconds at a time.

The following day, I telephoned the couple. The husband answered and I asked how his wife was. He replied, 'Fine, she's whipping batter to make pancakes for breakfast. Oh my God! She woke up this morning feeling fine and we both forgot that she couldn't move her arm.'

He had arrived home late and had forgotten all about our telephone talk, and so had not even mentioned the psychic healing idea to her. The arthritis pain was completely gone the next morning and – over the next fifteen years at least – did not reappear.

This was an unusually good response. Very often *no* observable result occurred, but enough cases of this sort happened to convince me that the phenomena were real.

Two questions immediately presented themselves. First, did the results obtained have anything to do with the shift in consciousness? Psychic healing ability has generally been attributed to a 'gift of grace', or to a personality quirk, depending on the viewpoint of the observer. It was possible I had been a 'natural' psychic healer (whatever that means) and simply never noticed or potentiated it until the research called it to my attention.

The obvious way to solve this problem was to see if the same procedure worked for others. Out of my own experience in learning to shift my consciousness – a learning procedure that took me a year and a half of about thirty hours work a week – I devised a training programme for others consisting of five days of ten to twelve hours' work a day. Of over 400 people who took this training course over the past ten years, my best estimate is that 80 to 90 per cent learned how to shift their consciousness in this way. Those who continued to practise it achieved the same kinds of positive biological changes that I had.[4]

It thus seemed clear that the shift in consciousness was one factor in the pattern that made up a 'successful' healing encounter, that made this type of transaction possible. This brought me squarely up against the second question: How did it work? What was going on?

The first clue came from a remark of George Bernard Shaw. He said that the shrine at Lourdes was the most blasphemous place on the face of the earth. When asked to explain his remark, he said that one only needed to look at what was there: mountains of wheelchairs, piles of crutches, 'but not a single wooden leg, glass eye or toupee!' This, said Shaw, implies a limitation on the power of God, and *that* is blasphemy.

It is of interest to note that in all the serious literature of psychic healing, there is not a single case of someone throwing away a wooden leg, a glass eye or a toupee. It becomes clear that, even under the best conditions, psychic healing has its limitations, which in itself is a clue to its nature. What it seems to boil down to is that psychic healing is limited to those kinds of results that the body can sometimes achieve on its own – the kind of thing we hear about in cases of 'spontaneous remission', sudden recoveries from various diseases without apparent cause. We hear of no such cases where a lost leg or eyeball was 'spontaneously' regenerated. Psychic healing appears to be limited to the same boundaries as the 'natural' healing abilities of the body under the best conditions.

The second clue came from a well-known concept in serious mysticism. This is the idea that a human being needs to be able to function in two different modes (at least) in order to achieve his fullest 'humanhood'. Plotinus used the analogy that a human being is like an amphibian that must live both on land and in the water in order to realize its full potential. Similarly, said Plotinus, a human must live both in the world of the 'One' and the world of the 'Many'. This idea is reflected in the fundamental convictions of every serious school of mysticism or esoteric development.

The Indian mystic Ramakrishna said, for example, that a human being is like a frog. In youth it lives (like a tadpole) in one medium – Water, or the Sensory Mode of organizing reality. Later, 'when the tail of ignorance drops off', it needs both land and water – the Sensory and the Unitary Mode – to fully attain its potentials.

The idea that began to develop at this point was furthered by a report made by Alexis Carrell, the great physiologist, who had set out to study what he called 'miraculous healing'. He observed what happened to an open and visible cancer when, in the course of a successful psychic healing, it underwent complete regression.

Carrell stated that sometimes a tumour undergoes 'spontaneous regression'. When it does this, it follows a well-known course. There is a change in its blood distribution, the formation of certain types of fibrous tissue, etc. The tumour he was observing, said Carrell, followed exactly that course of development, but many times faster than he had ever heard of before.

Putting these two ideas together, a concept began to emerge. None of us do anything as well as we possibly can. Whether we are talking about climbing a rope, understanding a book, discriminating wines, or making love, we can learn to do it better. We operate far below our potential. In healing ourselves, this is also true. Although we all use our self-healing abilities (as when we cut ourselves and the body heals the cut), we use them at a level of efficiency far below their potential. In psychic healing, the situation is temporarily changed by the healer-healee interaction, so that the healee is better able to use his self-healing abilities. This would explain the observation of Shaw. There are no wooden legs at Lourdes because the self-healing abilities (in contrast to those of lobsters) cannot regenerate a leg. *Psychic healing can only work up to the level of the self-healing abilities at their best.* All the data of the best reported cases would corroborate this hypothesis.

How did the healer-healee interaction change the situation to permit this? It seemed to me that this was best dealt with by the concept from mysticism that human beings needed to express themselves through a number of modes of organizing reality in order to attain their fullest humanhood. All of us, according to the various esoteric schools, are expert in the use of Sensory Mode – the mode by means of which we deal so effectively with the world of things accessible to the senses. The part of us that needs this expression is well satisfied. But the part of us that needs to express itself in the Clairvoyant or Unitary Mode, the way of the One, the mode of construing the world in which everything flows into everything else and no one is left outside, this part of us tends to be unsatisfied and undernourished. We are in a weakened condition, unable to use our self-healing abilities to their fullest. The specialized interaction of psychic healing changes this. The healer moves into the Unity Mode of construing the universe, with the healee as focus. He changes the metaphysical system of explaining and dealing with reality.

If conditions are right (and we know very little about what that means), the healee joins in, nourishes a part of himself that is undernourished, and is, for a time, more complete and better able to use his own self-healing abilities. The solution to the problem of how psychic healing works that I arrived at was that there was no such thing as psychic healing. There was only self-healing, but that this sometimes could be potentiated by the action of the healer. Theoretically, two people were in a certain state that included the healer's act of changing of his mode of organizing reality. A transaction occurred between the two that changed this state. The new state was sometimes obviously beneficial to the healee. There is no research that throws light on its effect on the healer.[5]

I do not intend here to discuss in detail the research programme and the training procedures in psychic healing. This was described extensively in my book, *The Medium, the Mystic and the Physicist,*[6] and further explicated in the work by Goodrich[7] and by Winston.[8]

Certain aspects that are particularly relevant to this book, however, do need to be presented here.

1. In all the many hundreds of healing encounters I and the people in the training groups participated in, there was never developed any ability to tell in advance which ones would result in medically unexpected positive biological changes, and which would not. We observed these changes taking place shortly after the healings quite often (my best estimate is about 15 to 20 per cent of the time), but could never predict in advance any specific healing.

A woman I knew well, admired and liked, asked me to do a healing with her. She had low back pain due to muscle spasm. Medical examination had shown no pathology. This is a type of problem that has, in our experience, frequently responded very well to psychic healing. During an afternoon, I worked several times with her. I achieved the Unity Mode with her as focus several times. It was a very moving experience for both of us. Afterwards we both felt somewhat shaken up, but also calm, and relaxed. There were some real telepathic exchanges during the process – similar atypical image had come to both our minds. There was no change in the low back pain then or in the several weeks following.

We know something about the conditions that were likely to produce positive biological results. However, all these conditions were present in the above case. We could train healers so that they could achieve results. We could show that with serious practice they would achieve these results more often. We could identify characteristics of the healee that would affect the likelihood of healing taking place. What we gradually came to understand, however, was that we could never predict in any single case. We are dealing, in psychic healing, with ideographic science, not nomothetic science. Therefore, when we finally know enough, we will be able to show *after* each psychic healing why it did or did not produce positive biological changes. We will never be able to make accurate predictions in the specific case.

2. We must deal with the observables found in the Realm of Consciousness and the Realm of Molar (Meaningful) Behaviour. These include 'purpose'. This has been widely observed by psychic healers in the past. As Stewart Grayson, an experienced and serious healer, put it: 'Feeling is the fuel behind the healing.' Every major healer has stressed that there must be *purpose, caring, love,* behind the healing; that it cannot be done mechanically. The purpose of both healer and healee in participating in the encounter must be seen as a vital part of the process.

3. Since space is not an observable in the Realm of Consciousness, we should expect that it would not be an observable in psychic healing. And this is the case. What can be done at a distance of one centimetre can also be done at a distance of a thousand kilometres. This is even true in those types of psychic healing – such as the 'laying on of hands' – in which it seems obvious that we are dealing with a local interaction. Some of our healers felt that they obtained their best results – indeed, sometimes their only results – when they held their hands over the damaged areas and 'perceived', 'hallucinated', a flow of 'healing energy' passing between their palms and through the damaged area (what we have elsewhere called Type 2 healing). These healers were asked to repeat the procedure some distance (up to many miles) from the healee and *imagine* that the damaged areas were between their palms. The results in the two cases (the damaged areas actually between their hands, and imagined between their hands) were about the same.

4. The psychic healers trained by this method who have kept up their practice have been in much demand. A constant flow of reported cases has come in from them. Many of these have

reported positive, medically unexpected, results. We have thus shown that a psychic ability can be trained so that it is actually useful. This is in spite of the fact that we can never, in principle, predict which case will be successful and which will not. It is by understanding more about the relevant conditions that we can increase the frequency with which desired results are obtained. We can make hypotheses and test them. We can increase our understanding so long as we are clear about in what realms of experience we are working, and that we are dealing with ideographic and not nomothetic science. In theory it should be possible to follow the same type of procedure with telepathy, clairvoyance and precognition.

The healing training seminars referred to in this chapter have, in the past years, been largely taught by Dr Joyce Goodrich and her Consciousness Research and Training Project. She continues to be quite successful in teaching people, including many with no previous psychic experience, to be effective as psychic healers.

12
CONCLUSIONS AND OVERTURE

As we look at the field of psi-occurrences, the strange and fascinating domain of the 'paranormal', it is almost impossible not to be immediately struck by the human paradox it implies.

There is no question now that the data is real. The very least we can say about it is that individuals sometimes have information that they did not obtain through the 'ordinary' route of the senses. No one who objectively investigates the field can fail to come to this conclusion. It is a startling and clearly very important fact. Obviously it implies that there is very much we do not know about the nature of man and his relationship to others and to the cosmos. This new information, the new ideas that Type B perception implies, may well be what we desperately need in a time when, using our old ideas to the full, we cannot stop killing each other or poisoning our planet. Floyd Matson wrote: 'For if it is true, in general, that ideas have consequences, then man's ideas about man have the most far reaching consequences of all.'[1]

And yet, there is very little interest in this area. In the whole world it is doubtful if there are twenty-five full-time research specialists working in it, and only a double handful of part-time workers. The major scientific journals come out in editions of less than 3000 copies each. The British Society for Psychical Research averages less than 100 people in attendance at its London lectures. Both the British and American Societies are in the process of becoming smaller and smaller, and are doing less and less. The few workers in the field with a wide view and a sense of its excitement and potential find themselves struggling uphill in a small scientific community that has largely lost these qualities. The research in this field has for the most part become divorced from human interests and concerns. We have studied smaller and smaller details with more and more precise techniques. Focusing increasingly on the details, and less and less on the larger picture, we have successfully applied our energy and intelligence to make molehills out of mountains.

And all this in spite of the fact that, again and again in our work, we are brought face to face with the larger issues of meaning. What does it mean to be human? What is the human condition?

> A woman ... dreamed in California on 20 January 1945 that her only child, then serving in the Pacific with the American navy, came into the kitchen where she was working, dropped his dripping naval uniform into the washtub, took her in his arms and said, 'Isn't this terrible? This is the one thing I hoped you would never have to hear.' She did not know what the terrible thing was. They went into the living room, and he sat on her knee, sobbing, till at last she rocked him to sleep, a child again, in her arms. Six days later a chaplain from the local naval base came to tell her that her son's ship had been torpedoed on the night of 20 January, and that his name was among the missing, blown to bits.[2]

The cases presented in this book are typical of those known to everyone with experience in the field. We have so many of them, carefully studied and evaluated, that the professional journals have stopped printing them. And each one of them says something important about human interrelatedness. In addition, we have a great many laboratory studies, done with the careful techniques of modern science. Both kinds of data say the same thing: people often have information that they did not receive through the senses. Nothing we know of (except, perhaps, our own attitudes) can completely separate us from each other.

Put this last point differently, and you define the essence and importance of this field. The study of Type B perception (psychical research and parapsychology) is the study of *how individuals cannot be fully separated from each other.* Not by space, time, walls, Faraday cages, the curve of the planet, perhaps not even by death itself. Other fields study how individuals are separate and how they affect each other through various modes of communication. Our field stresses our non-separate nature – non-separate from each other and from all of nature.

This ONENESS is there, but demonstrates its existence only rarely – just often enough to let us be sure it is there and is real. Our oneness is as real – neither more or less – as is our individuality. We know a great deal about our individuality and how we interact. We know very little about our oneness. Our individuality is as obvious and commonplace as our ordinary communication. Our oneness is as rare and subtle as our Type B perceptions. Both indicate a part of what it means to be human.

Perhaps – as many esoteric schools have insisted – it is the lack of acceptance of this oneness part of us that has crippled our race so that, with the highest capacity for good in us and our behaviour, with thousands of demonstrations all through history that human beings have the potential for living lives of love, loyalty, steadfastness, *caritas,* joy, decency and the other characteristics of *virtu,* we go on tearing at ourselves and each other like rats in a poisoned cage.

This is the goal of our field: to bring to light a part of us long hidden – and yet reported repeatedly all through human history – so that we can help bring our race closer to completeness, and help it move towards full humanity.

As we look at the sorry tale of progress in our field in the past fifty to hundred years, we can see how many unverbalized and unexamined assumptions have helped block our progress. It is these that this exploration of ideas has attempted to bring to light and to clarify.

It is time to formulate conclusions. The following is a summary of the points I have tried to make in this book:

1. Normal perceptions and paranormal perceptions (Type A and Type B perceptions) are equally mysterious. We do not understand how the information (in Type B perception) 'jumps' from Mary's consciousness to the consciousness of Josephine. The academic psychologist (studying Type A perception) does not understand how the information 'jumps' from Jack's nervous system to Jack's consciousness. Parapsychologists have no need to be apologetic about their field. We may be studying phenomena that are less often detected than those of the academic psychologist, but they are no more mysterious.

2. Modern science works by choosing a particular slice of reality (a 'domain') and asking what are the observables found in it. We then ask what are the relationships among these observables, and what entities (constructs) we need to posit to 'carry' them. If we see points of light in the night sky, we find observables such as direction, brightness, periodicity, heat and distance and we posit the existence of a 'star' to carry these observables. We ask what are the relationships among the observables and constructs, and what guiding principles (such as space, time, causality, etc.) we need to define in order to make these relationships coherent. These define for us the 'realm of experience' into which the particular domain fits (in this case, the realm of the very large and fast – the Relativity Domain).

Type B perceptions – psi-gamma events – are observed in two realms: the Realm of Consciousness and the Realm of Meaningful Behaviour. Literally, we are aware of them, and only aware of them, when someone knows or feels something, or someone does something. If we are going to behave scientifically in our search for understanding, we must follow certain procedures. We must ask what other observables we find in these realms, and what the relationships are among these other observables and Type B perceptions. We must then ask how we need to define guiding principles in these realms. We must stop wasting time over such questions as, 'What is psi?' Modern science asks questions about relationships, not about basic definitions of this sort.

3. In each realm, we ask what the guiding principles are. We then define the basic limiting principles of the realm. We then find that there is no such thing as a 'paranormal' experience in this realm. 'Paranormal' means 'impossible' – something that violates the basic limiting principles of the realm – *and impossible events do not happen.* If we observe one, we first check our eyeglasses, and then recheck the guiding principles we are using in the particular realm of experience in which we observed the event. If our eyeglasses are adequate, then our definitions of guiding principles are faulty.

4. Following this procedure, it is entirely possible to study scientifically the large scale Type B perceptions that first excited our interest in this field.

5. In the realms in which we observe Type B perceptions, a repeatable experiment to predict individual behaviour is impossible. We cannot say that 'Given conditions X, Y and Z, then Thomas Jones will have a Type B perception.' Or that, 'Given conditions X, Y and Z, Mr Henry Smith will have a 40 per cent chance of having a Type B perception.' This type of experiment – a 'psi-producing machine' – is impossible in principle, and we might as well accept the fact and stop wasting time and energy trying to produce it, then becoming apologetic and guilty that we cannot. Certain devices – such as a perpetual motion machine that works, or a psi-producing machine – are not possible to produce, and that is that.

In spite of all the papers, discussions and conferences on the 'Problem of Repeatability in Parapsychology', there is no such problem. That is why it has not been solved – you cannot solve false problems. In ideographic science, there is no such possibility of specific event predictability, any more than there is in science in the quantum realm.

6. We can, however, perform experiments of the type that state, 'in a W-type group, given X, Y and Z conditions, Type B perceptions will be more common when these conditions are not present.' Or ones that state, 'Type B perceptions having certain functions (maintaining certain roles, stabilizing relationships, etc.) will be more common than Type B perceptions that do not have these functions.' There are many testable hypotheses of this sort we can legitimately make.

7. The basic unit in studying Type B perception is the 'transaction' of modern communication theory, not the 'message' of information theory. Part of our problems in research in this field is that we have been using long-outdated models of communication. We have been using 'action' or 'reaction' models, not 'transactional' models.

8. Since Type B perceptions are observed in the Realm of Consciousness and the Realm of Meaningful Behaviour, we must use the guiding principles of these realms to design our experiments and theories. In nearly all our work, however, we have been using the definitions from the sensory realm. Typical is our definition of 'space' in our field. We have nearly always used the definition from the sensory realm for data observed in other

realms. This has been a major reason for our obtaining erratic and sporadic results. It has also helped lead to the theoretical mess in which we still find ourselves.

9. When we apply the proper definition of 'space' to Type B perceptions, the major question we have been asking ourselves in our field – 'How does the information get across the space between Joe and Jim, or between Jim and the target object?' – reveals itself to be a false and meaningless question. The reason we have not been able to find an answer to it is because you cannot find answers to meaningless questions. All you can find are headaches.

10. A major observable in the realms in which we observe Type B perceptions is 'purpose'. Leibniz wrote: 'Minds act in accordance with the laws of final causes. Bodies act in accordance with the laws of efficient causes.' Due to the preconceptions we para-psychologists have brought to our work, this has been largely ignored. This has helped lead us to the kind of results we would have obtained if we had ignored the observable 'temperature' in the study of thermodynamics.

11. The correct way to 'order' our data in this field is on the basis of the *histories* of the persons or objects involved, not on the basis of their *properties.* When a science orders its data on the wrong basis, as we have been doing, its results are extremely spotty and unpredictable. Furthermore, until it achieves a proper ordering, it will not be granted scientific respectability.

12. The correct model of our science – due to the realms in which our data are observed – is that of ideographic science, not that of nomothetic science. This means, among other things, that we must make major changes in our definitions of causation and predictability. In ideographic science, one can demonstrate that an event that has taken place *had* to happen, and why. One cannot, however, predict a specific event in the future. This is not due to a limitation of knowledge, but is as much a limitation in principle as is the Heisenberg Limitation in the quantum realm. Continued attempts to treat our data as if they fell under the model of nomothetic science (in which specific events can be predicted, repeatable experiments can be devised, etc.) will continue to lead us around in circles.

What I have attempted to do in this book is to explore the reasons why psychical research and parapsychology have shown such a dismal lack of progress over the last fifty years, and what can be done about this lack. Once we stopped looking at our data in their own terms and started looking at them in terms of preconceived theory from another realm of experience, we were deeply mired. It is certainly true that the model we chose, that of nineteenth-century physics and mechanics, has led to tremendous and dramatic progress in those fields. But scientific progress in one field is not made by using the methods, research instruments, tools and concepts from another. One does not get very far in the study of hearing by using research instruments designed for, and relevant to, the study of vision, no matter what marvellous results the researchers in optics have achieved.

Sigmund Koch, the leading historian of psychology, wrote:

> Psychology [and I would add, parapsychology as one branch of psychology] is necessarily the most philosophy-sensitive discipline in the entire gamut of disciplines that claim empirical status. We cannot discriminate a so-called variable, pose a research question, choose or invent a method, stipulate a psycho-technology, without making strong presumptions of philosophical cast about the nature of our human subjects.[3]

As we have become increasingly more precise in our methodology, we have increasingly ignored the philosophical assumptions we have been making. We have adapted sets of assumptions that were valid for other realms of experience, in particular those adapted to, and only valid for, the sensory realm. This is a realm in which we do not observe Type B perceptions, and in which they can neither happen nor in which they can be explained. Ernst Cassirer has warned us: 'The science of culture and of individual behaviour cannot renounce anthropomorphism and anthropocentrism.'[4] In our effort to be 'scientific', we have forgotten that we are dealing with human beings, and that they behave in far different ways and with far different motivations than do computers, machines, or anything else we observe in the sensory realm.

When we look at the data from psychical research in its own terms, and without preconceptions as to what it should be or what kind of theories should be devised to fit it, we can see it for what it is, and we find theories to make it coherent. Until, however, we cease to hold on so stubbornly to ideas taken in advance, we shall be unable to achieve these goals.

David Kahn, in an important, but long-forgotten paper, has clearly described the crisis of parapsychology. He writes of Galileo:[5]

> The next case history, which has been carefully analyzed by F. S. C. Northrop in one of his essays, bears directly on the heart of the psi problem as I see it. Galileo became disturbed by the movement of projectiles, which he came to realize did not behave as they should according to Aristotle's physics. This, like our spontaneous cases, was the problem that first presented itself in nature. Had Galileo been Baconian, he would have observed all possible varieties of moving projectiles, as we collect cases of psi, and, like us, might still be collecting. As a Cartesian, he would have returned to certain basic Aristotelian principles of nature, as did his predecessors, and he would have only compounded his dilemma. For deductions from the principle that force is that which gives objects their motion or velocity – a principle which seemed confirmed on innumerable occasions – would have necessarily been erroneous. Hypothesis formulation limited to projectiles, after Cohen and Nagel, would certainly have been equally fruitless.
>
> Instead of these traditional approaches Galileo revealed his genius by first concerning himself with transforming the problem in nature into its correct terms. This, according to John Dewey, *must be the initial step in every inquiry,* and if the correct analysis of the problem is made at the very beginning, then the traditional methods will be found to work, when the time comes to use them in the later stages of inquiry.
>
> Galileo's analysis of the problem compelled him to believe, despite the fact his initial interest was aroused by the peculiarly unnatural behaviour of projectiles, that the real problem lay elsewhere. He saw that the concept of force – though there was no more deeply ingrained concept in his contemporary physics – was erroneous. This brilliant insight led finally to his experiments designed to redefine force, without respect to projectiles. When his new concept of force was developed – that force is that which gives acceleration to bodies – he found not only did he understand projectiles, but also had a profound and revolutionary insight into mechanics in general, thus setting the historical stage for Newton and all of modern science.

It is revolutionary thinking like that of Galileo that the present state of our field calls us to essay. We must try to reformulate the problem in its correct terms. It has been the attempt of this book to begin that task. Whether or not this particular formulation proves to be the most fruitful for this period, there is no doubt that the core of our social ills lies in our unwillingness to re-examine our current biases about the nature of Man. It is surely time to begin.

NOTES AND REFERENCES

Introduction

[1] Stevens, W. O., *Psychics and Common Sense,* Dutton, New York 1953, p. 9.

[2] Schrodinger, E., *Science and Humanism; Physics in Our Times,* Cambridge University Press, 1961, p. 25.

1: The Background of the Problem

[1] Some of the above is a paraphrase of part of Mundle, C. W. E., 'Strange Facts in Search of a Theory', *Proc. S.P.R.,* vol. 56, 1973, pp. 1-20. Mundle further suggests that in view of the anxiety and outrage produced in materialists at the idea of the existence of the 'non-physical', many modern people are as terrified at the idea of finding that they have a soul as a medieval person would have been at the idea he did not.

[2] Gurney, E., Myers, F. W. H., Podmore, F., *Phantasms of the Living* (Abridged Edition), London, Kegan, Paul, Trench, Trubner, 1918, pp. 132-133.

[3] Tyrrell, G. N. M., *Apparitions,* Pantheon, N.Y., 1953.

[4] Ducasse, C. J., *Paranormal Phenomenon, Science, and Life after Death,* Parapsychological Monographs No. 8, Parapsychology Foundation, New York City, 1967, p. 31.

[5] Grattan, Guinness, I. (ed.), *Psychical Research,* Aquarian Press, Northamptonshire, 1982.

[6] Story told by both participants to various members of the family and others. Both men, one later a physician, the other later a lawyer and the

President of the Society for Ethical Culture, felt up to the present that 'mental telepathy' must exist even though both were strong agnostics and rationalists and felt that the idea contradicted everything else that they believed.

[7] Gill, D., 'Miracle in a Dish', *Modern Maturity,* June-July, 1983, p. 3.

[8] Murphy, G., in Rhine, J. B., and Brier, R., *Parapsychology Today,* Citadel, N.Y., 1968, p. 127.

[9] This abandonment of the study of consciousness was also a part of a major thrust of the thought of the twentieth century. In Pitrim Sorokin's words: 'We have seen that modern sensate culture emerged with a major belief that true reality and true value was mainly or exclusively sensory. Anything that was supersensory was either doubtful as a reality or fictitious as a value. It either did not exist, or being unperceivable by the senses, amounted to the non-existent. . . . Since true reality and true values were thought to be sensory, anything that was supersensory, from the conception of God to the mind of man, anything that was non-material, that could not in the way of daily experience be seen, heard, tasted, touched or smelled, had to be declared unreal, non-existent and of no value.' Sorokin, P., *The Crisis of Our Age,* N.Y., E. P. Dutton, 1941, p. 311.

[10] Koch, S., 'Psychology Cannot be a Coherent Science', *Psychology Today,* vol. 3, no. 4, 1965, p. 14.

[11] Bertalanffy, L. V., 'Chance or Law?', in Koestler, A., and Smythies, J. R. (eds.), *Beyond Reductionism,* Beacon Press, Boston, 1971, p. 59.

[12] Skinner, B. F., *Science and Human Behavior,* Macmillan, N.Y., 1953, p. 447.

[13] Part of the basic problem of parapsychology has been an idea that took root in philosophy in antiquity. This is that there is a natural division of philosophy into logic, physics and ethics. (Kant recognized this and declared it to be valid as 'it conforms to the nature of things and permits no improvement'.) This is an unspoken assumption in our thinking. Parapsychology does not fit into logic or ethics. Perforce we tend to think of it as belonging to physics. (Part of the above is taken from Cassirer, E., *The Logic of the Humanities,* Yale University Press, New Haven, Conn., 1960, p. 3.)

[14] Orne, M. T., 'On the Social Psychology of the Psychological Experiment', *American Psychologist,* 1962, 17, pp. 776-783.

[15] Brunswik, E., 'Representative Design and Probabilistic Theory in a Functional Psychology', *Psychology Review,* 1955, 62, pp. 193-217.

[16] Harre, R., and Secord, P. F., *The Explanation of Social Behaviour,* Academic Press, London, 1972.

[17] Gadlin, H., and Ingle, G., 'Through the One-Way Mirror: The Limits of Experimental Self-Reflection', *American Psychologist,* 1975, 30, pp. 1003-1010.

[18] Berkowitz, C., and Donnerstein, E., 'External Validity is more than Skin Deep: Some Answers to Questions of Laboratory Experiments', *American Psychologist,* 1982, 37, pp. 245-257.

2. The 'Normal' and the 'Paranormal'

[1] Ogden, C. K., *The Meaning of Psychology,* New York, Harper, 1926, p. 174.

[2] Murphy, G., 'Psychical Research and Personality', *Proc. S.P.R., 1949-1952,* 49, pp. 1-15, p. 6.

[3] –, 'Psychology and Psychical Research', *Proc. S.P.R. 1953,* 50, pp. 21-50, p. 33.

[4] Warcollier, R., *Mind to Mind,* New York, Collier, 1963.

[5] Beloff, J., 'Trying to Make Sense Out of the Paranormal', *Proc. S.P.R.,* 1975, 56, pp. 173-195, p. 177.

[6] Rhine, J. B., 'On Parapsychology and the Nature of Man', in Hook, S. (ed.), *Dimensions of Mind,* New York, Collier, 1960, pp. 74-84, p. 75.

[7] Ducasse, C. J., *Nature, Mind and Death,* Open Coast Publ. Co., 1951.

[8] Thouless, R. H. and Weisner, B. P., 'The Psi Processes in Normal and Paranormal Perception', *Proc. S.P.R., XLVIII,* 1947, p. 180.

[9] Moncrief, M. M., *The Clairvoyant Theory of Perception,* Faber and Faber, London, 1951.

[10] Eddington, A. S., *Science and the Unseen World,* New York, Macmillan, 1937, p. 34.

[11] Holroyd, S., *Psi and the Consciousness Explosion,* New York, Taplinger Pub., 1977, p. 21.

[12] Sinnott, E. W., *The Bridge of Life,* New York, Simon and Schuster, 1966, p. 168.

[13] Weyer, E. M., 'A Unit Concept of Consciousness', *Psychology Review, XVII,* 1910, pp. 301-318.

[14] Joad, C. E. M., book review, *The New Statesman and Nation,* vol. 23, 1948. Quoted in Ehrenwald, J., *New Dimensions in Psychoanalysis,* p. 213.

[15] G. N. M. Tyrrell analyzed Type B perceptions into two parts – a paranormal part and a 'normal' part. He called them Stage 1 and Stage 2. He showed that Stage 2 obeyed all the laws of the psychology of perceptions and regarded stage 1 as essentially unanalyzable. (Tyrrell, G. N. M., 'The Modus Operandi of Paranormal Cognition', *Proc. S.P.R.,* 48, 1946, pp. 65-120.)

This is a somewhat more sophisticated approach than one generally finds in the field. However, Tyrrell did not make the next step and point out that normal cognition also has two stages, sensory-neural and conscious, and that different methods of analysis are needed for each.

3: The New Development in Science

[1] Ellison, A. J., Presidential Address, 1982, 'Psychical Research after 100 years. What do we Really Know?', *Proc. S.P.R.,* vol. 56, 1982, pp. 384-398.

[2] Newton had emphasized that the idea of a unified cosmos with all its processes subject to the same law arose from theological considerations. *Principia: General Scholium to Book 3,* and his letters to Bentley.

[3] The influence of this shadow skeleton is often very strong. When Kepler, who developed the idea that the Earth and planets revolve around the sun, was trying to understand the paths of the bodies in the solar system, one of the criteria he used was 'What geometrical shapes would a perfect God prefer?'

[4] Long before this, Giordano Bruno had warned us to be cautious in this type of reasoning:

> We must fix limits to our expectations of evidence from the senses. We admit their testimony only on things perceptible to them; and even then not without appeal, unless their judgment be controlled by reason. Think of how variable they are in determining such a thing as the horizon. When we know from experiment how readily we are deceived by them in matters pertaining to the surface of this globe on which we live, how much more should we suspect them in what they tell us of the limits of the starry dome. (Bruno, *De l'Infinito Universo e Mundi*)

[5] Pagels, H., *The Cosmic Code,* New York, Simon and Schuster, 1982, p. 18.

[6] Only after that greatest triumph of engineering in history – the Industrial Revolution – could we have believed that it was a reasonable idea that creation, evolution, the mind and society, all worked on purely mechanical principles. 'It was mathematics and mathematical natural science which fashioned the ideal of knowledge of this age and aside from geometry, analysis and mechanics, there appeared to be no room for any other truly rigorous scientific inquiry.' (Cassirer, E., *The Logic of the Humanities,* Yale University Press, New Haven, Conn., 1960, p. 4.)

[7] This is true to a much greater degree than is obvious at first sight. We have been so impressed with the accomplishments of the engineer that we have borrowed his metaphors and used them everywhere. As L. P. Jacks observed, we ask our thinkers to 'reconstruct' our society, morals and government, and to 'be constructive' as an engineer is when he produces a skyscraper. We feel we need to 'build a bridge' between science and ethics, and between the US and the USSR. We organize everything into 'problem' and 'solution' (neither of these words is found in the Bible). 'Whether human life is amenable to these methods is a question that does not trouble us. We hardly see the meaning of the question, so hard-set are we in our engineering proclivities.' (Jacks, L. P., *The Revolt Against Mechanism,* 1934, Macmillan, p. 33.)

In Oswald Spengler's words, 'The present age is the age of the engineer.' Jacks (p. 48) suggests a new commandment, 'Render unto life the things that are Life's, and unto mechanism . . .'.

> For about a hundred years down to the end of the last World War, the trend among psychologists, physiologists and philosophers was toward an uncompromising physicalism. Into this cast-iron mold all facts and theories had to be fitted and trimmed. Toward the close of the century, the faith in a purely materialistic universe had become as sacrosanct among scientists as the belief in a spiritual world had been throughout the dark ages; and in science, as in religion, faith often piles up mountains which it afterwards has to remove. (Burt, C., *Psychology and Psychical Research,* p. 7 ff.)

> The rise of mechanical conceptions of the universe in Copernicus', Galileo's and Newton's orderly explanations of the movements of celestial bodies and terrestrial objects subjected to experiments made it appear to the Eighteenth Century that the universe was one great homogeneous system allowing no real credibility for mental events independent of physical events. (Leeds, M., and Murphy, G. *The Normal and the Paranormal,* Scarecrow Press, Metuchen, N.J., 1980, p. xv.)

[8] In evaluating the possibility of a new descriptive model for a realm of experience, we must beware that the model so forcibly present to our senses is relevant only to the realm of experience accessible to the senses. As an example of this, I might point out that matter, so steadfast, solid and reliable in the sensory realm is something very different in the quantum realm. In Bertrand Russell's words, 'a piece of matter has become not a persistent thing with various states, but a system of interrelated events'. Russell, B., Introduction to Lange, *A History of Materialism,* London, Kegan Paul, 1925, p. 11. 'One part of physics must be governed by differential equations, while there is another part that is dealt with by quantum theory – in which this whole apparatus is inappropriate.' Russell, B., *The Analysis of Matter,* New York, Harcourt Brace, 1927.

One of the earliest statements of the existence and importance of different realms of experience was made by the philosopher Immanual Kant. His doctrine demands a difference between the world of the senses (*mundus sensibilis*) and the world of intelligence (*mundus intelligibilis*), a 'dualism between nature and freedom'.

[9] As Jacob Bronowski put it: 'Cause and effect are large scale operations.' *The Common Sense of Science,* Boston, Harvard University Press, 1978, p. 76.

[10] Bohr, N., *Atomic Theory and the Description of Nature,* Cambridge University Press, 1934, p. 109.

[11] This point (and many others in this book) was called to my attention by the physicist-philosopher Henry Margenau.

[12] Sinnott, E. W., *The Bridge of Life,* Simon and Schuster, New York, 1966, p. 72.

[13] One of the hardest things for us to realize and accept today is that there is no concept of space that is more basic, more *true,* than all the others: that there is no 'correct' concept. The space of the painter, the architect, the sculptor, the artilleryman, the astronomer, the quantum scientist, and the lover are all different; none is more correct than any of the others.

[14] Eddington, A. S., quoted by G. N. M. Tyrrell, *Grades of Significance,* London, Rider and Company, 1930, p. 56.

[15] Crumbaugh, J. C., 'The Significance of Gestalt Psychology for the Problem of Immortality', *J.A.S.P.R.,* April 1956, 50, pp. 59, 65.

[16] Murphy, G., 'Three Papers on the Survival Problem', *J.A.S.P.R.,* 1950.

> The cosmological law and order of classical physics – what Ernst Cassirer called 'the iron ring of necessity that anchors our every thought and action' – has been thoroughly subverted by the succession of revolutions in physics itself; and the traditional fixed boundary between Subjectivity and Objectivity, between Appearance and Reality, has been so often penetrated and overrun to be virtually undefended if not indefensible: the Maginot Line of the old order. (Matson, F. W., *The Idea of Man.* Dell, New York 1970, p. 3.)

[17] Rosen, S., 'Psi-Modelling and the Psycho-physical Question: An Epistomological Crisis', *Parapsychology Review,* vol. 14, no. 1, Jan.-Feb. 1983, pp. 17-24, p. 17.

[18] Rhine, L., *ESP in Life and Laboratory,* Macmillan, New York, 1967.

[19] Stevenson, I., *Telepathic Impressions,* University of Virginia Press, Charlottesville, Virginia, 1970.

[20] Rushton, W. A. H., 'First Sight, Second Sight', *Proc. S.P.R.,* 55, 1971, pp. 177-188, p. 177. In ESP drawing tests of the Warcollier type and W. Carrington type, the 'hit' sometimes resembles the form of the target, sometimes its meaning. We are not dealing with a special type of sense perception: we are dealing with an event in consciousness – a psychological construct. In this it is similar to other events in consciousness.

[21] Ayer, A. J., in Flew, A., *Body, Mind and Death,* Macmillan, 1954, p. 19.

[22] The material in this chapter is discussed at much greater length and detail in LeShan, L., and Margenau, H., *Einstein's Space and Van Gogh's Sky: Physical Reality and Beyond,* Macmillan, New York, 1982; Harvester, 1983.

4: The Realm of Consciousness

[1] Eddington, A. S., *Science and the Unseen World,* Macmillan, New York, 1937, p. 54.

[2] Titchener, E. B., *An Outline of Psychology,* New York, Macmillan, 1896, p. 2.

[3] John Locke, quoted in *ibid.,* p. 2.

[4] Some of the following is, I believe, a paraphrase of some remarks of William James.

[5] Burt, C., *Psychology and Psychical Research,* S.P.R., London, 1968, p. 64.

[6] Freud, S., *Civilisation and Its Discontents* (tr. J. Rivere), Hogarth, London, 1949, p. 20.

[7] Titchener, *op. cit.,* p. 4. We might, of course, say that no such entities as 'things' exist anywhere, that even a rock is a process. There is some truth in this, but not very much. It is perfectly clear to all of us that there is a vast difference between a rock lying there as a thing and the process of the rock flying through the air and hitting us on the head. One is a thing, and one is a process, and we are in no doubt as to which is which. If we want to describe a thing as a very slowed-down process, we are within our intellectual and philosophical rights, but except for some special lines on inquiry, it is probably not going to get us very far.

[8] Sidis, B., *The Foundation of Normal and Abnormal Psychology,* R. C. Badger, Toronto, 1914, p. 113.

[9] Sherrington, 'Man on his Nature', quoted in Eccles, Sir. J., *Facing Reality,* Berlin, Springer-Verlag, 1970, p. 59.

[10] Ogden, C. K., *The Meaning of Psychology,* New York, Harper and Bros., 1926, p. 158.

[11] Vesey, G., 'What Defines Privacy', in Josephson, B. D., and Ramachandra, V. S., *Consciousness and the Physical World,* Permagon Press, New York, 1980, p. 21.

[12] Munsterberg, H., *Psychology and Life,* New York, Houghton-Mifflin, 1899.

[13] Bergson, H., 'Presidential Address', *Proceedings S.P.R., LVIII,* pp. 157-175, p. 164. For a fuller and more scientifically rigorous discussion of this point, see Margenau, H., *The Nature of Physical Reality,* Oxbow Press, New Haven, Conn., 1977.

[14] Haynes, R., in Koestler, A., *The Roots of Coincidence,* Random House, New York, 1973, p. 147.

[15] The idea that quantification in the Realm of Consciousness and in that of Molar Behaviour is limited to general classes (such as Very Probable, Probable, Improbable, Very Improbable), and cannot in principle be carried further, is similar to Carnap's concept of 'degree of confirmation' in which actual computation of the probabilities cannot be carried out in the real world, but only in idealized (and very simple cases). See Carnap, R., 'Probability as a Guide in life', *Journal of Philosophy,* 44, 1947, pp. 141-148, and 'The Two Concepts of Probability', *Philosophical and Phenomological Research,* 5, 1945, pp. 513-522.

[16] James, W., *The Principles of Psychology,* Dover, New York, 1950 (originally published 1890), p. 230.

[17] Ibid., p. 230.

[18] Bergson, *op. cit.*, p. 159, p. 10. One might be tempted here to see something like the 'Jubilee' theory of the ancient Greeks – that every so many years the entire universe spins completely around and we are back exactly where we started; everything will be identical with what it is at this moment. This is probably philosophically permissible, although today we would insist on a much longer period than the 7000 years that the Greeks thought completed the jubilee. We would talk of 'infinity' and that in it all situations must repeat exactly. This may have some interesting metaphysical possibilities, but it seems extremely unlikely to be of much help to us in our search for greater understanding of the paranormal.

[19] Kierkegaard, S., *Repetition: An Essay in Experimental Psychology,* Harper Torch Books, New York 1964, p. 77.

[20] Brier, R., 'Methodology in Parapsychology and in Other Sciences', *Parap. Rev., vol. 4,* no. 1, Jan-Feb, 1973, p. 1.

[21] Koestler, A., in Beloff, J., *New Directions in Parapsychology,* Elek Science Press, London, 1974, p. 165 ff.

[22] This point is explored in some length by Paul Meehl in his *Clinical Versus Statistical Prediction,* University of Minnesota Press, Minneapolis, 1954. See also Sarbin, T. R., 'The Logic of Prediction in Psychology', *Psychol. Rev.,* 51, 1944, pp. 210-228.

[23] Quoted in James, W., *Essays in Radical Empiricism,* Longmans-Green, New York, 1912.

[24] Eisenbud, J., *Paranormal Foreknowledge,* Human Sciences Press, New York, 1982, p. 148.

[25] Cassirer, E., *An Essay on Man,* Yale University Press, New Haven, 1944, p. 11.

[26] Eddington, *op. cit.,* p. 53.

[27] Quoted in Zajonc, R. B., 'Feeling and Thinking: Preferences Need No Inferences', *American Psychologist,* 1980, 35, pp. 151-175, p. 160.

[28] This book is not the place to go into detail about the various aspects of the Realm of Consciousness. This has been done in greater depth elsewhere (LeShan, L., and Margenau, H., *Einstein's Space and Van Gogh's Sky: The Faces of Reality,* Macmillan, 1982; and Margenau, H., *The Miracle of Existence,* in press). In addition, there are now new books on the subject coming out, as well as some of the older literature such as William James' classic *Principles of Psychology,* vol. 1.

[29] Munsterberg, H., *op. cit.,* p. 54.

[30] Sidis, *op. cit.,* p. 24.

[31] This lack of 'space' in the Realm of Consciousness shows us why there are no 'objects' in this realm: 'The knowledge that a quantity is an unobservable does not result from the failure of results to observe it, but from "scrutinizing its definition" which is self-contradictory or in some other way "illogical".' (Rosenthal-Schneider, I., *Reality and Scientific*

Truth: Discussions with Einstein, von Laue and Planck, Wayne State University Press, Detroit, 1980, p. 122.) An 'object' is separate in space from other 'objects'. Where there is no space (and so no separation in it) there are no objects.

[32] Cox, W. E., 'Precognition: An Analysis', *J.A.S.P.R.*, 50. 1956, pp. 47-58.
[33] Quoted by duNouy, Lecomte, *Human Destiny,* Signet, New York, 1947, p. 41.
[34] Munsterberg, *op. cit.,* p. 56.
[35] Eisenbud, J., 'Psi and the Nature of Things', *International Journal of Parapsychology, vol. 5,* 1963, pp. 245-273, p. 265.
[36] Schrodinger, E., *Science and Humanism: Physics in Our Time,* Cambridge University Press, London, 1961, p. 63.
[37] Polanyi, M., *The Tacit Dimension,* Anchor, New York, 1967, p. 37.
[38] Eccles, J. C., *op. cit.,* p. 54.
[39] Penfield, W., *The Mystery of the Mind,* Princeton University Press, Princeton, N.J., 1975, p. xxv.
[40] Schrodinger, *op. cit.,* p. 29.
[41] Freud, S., *Some Additional Notes on Dream Association as a Whole,* 1915.
[42] Ehrenwald, J., *The ESP Hypothesis,* Basic Books, New York, 1978, p. 229.
[43] Bronowski, J., *The Common Sense of Science,* Harvard University Press, Cambridge, Mass., 1978, p. 48.
[44] West, D. J., and Fisk, G. W., 'A Dual Experiment with Clock Cards', *J.A.S.P.R.,* 37, 1953-1954, pp. 185-187.
[45] Beloff, J., 'J. B. Rhine and the Nature of Psi', *Journal of Parapsychology,* 55, 1981, pp. 41-54, p. 42.
[46] Cassirer, E., *The Logic of the Humanities,* Yale University Press, New Haven, Conn., 1960, p. 143.
[47] Bronowski, *op. cit.,* p. 48.
[48] *Ibid.,* p. 53.
[49] Another way of listing the differences between the 'physical' (the Realm of the Senses) and the 'mental' (the Realm of Consciousness) is presented by the philosopher, H. Feigl:

Mental	Physical
Subjective (Private)	Objective (Public)
Nonspatial	Spatial
Qualitative	Quantitative
Purposive	Mechanical
Mnemic	Non-Mnemic
Holistic	Atomistic
Emergent	Compositional
Intentional	'Blind', Non-Intentional

(Feigl, H., 'The "Mental" and the "Physical",' in Feigl, H., Scriven,

M., and Maxwell, G., *Minnesota Studies in the Philosophy of Science*, vol. 2, University of Minnesota Press, Minneapolis, 1963, p. 396.)

[50] In one way we are, in this book, going back to the Socratic conception of man. This is described by Ernst Cassirer: 'We cannot discover the nature of man in the same way as we detect the nature of physical things. Physical things may be described in terms of their objective properties, but man may be described and defined only in terms of his consciousness.' (Cassirer, E., *Essay on Man*, Doubleday-Anchor, New York 1954, p. 20.)

5: What Is Consciousness and Where Is It?

[1] James, W., *Principles of Psychology*, vol. 1, Henry Holt, New York, 1910, p. 185.

[2] *Ibid.*, p. 6.

[3] Pearson, K., *The Grammar of Science*, Meridian, New York, 1957, p. 272.

[4] If you want to have a little fun with this, look at a nearby wall and try to figure out where 'you', the 'inner self', the 'looker', is located. Then close both eyes and see how the location changes. Then look with one eye at a time and observe the movements. You will perceive the self moving around as you shift your visual apparatus.

[5] Jordan, P., 'New Trends in Physics', in *Proceedings of Four Conferences of Parapsychological Studies*, Parapsychology Foundation, New York, 1957, p. 16.

[6] 'But it behooves us to be very careful, and not to forget that we are dealing only with analogies, and that it is dangerous, not only with men but also with concepts, to drag them out of the region where they originated and have matured.' (Freud, *Civilization and its Discontents.*)

[7] Margenau, H., 'The Method of Science', in Margenau, H. (ed.), *Integrative Principles of Modern Thought*, Gordon and Breach, New York, 1972, p. 10.

[8] Penfield, W., *The Mystery of the Mind*, Princeton University Press, Princeton, N.J., 1975, p. 10. 'There is simply no distance to travel and no time span to jump.' (Beloff, J., 'On Trying to Make Sense of the Paranormal', *Proc. S.P.R.*, vol. 86, pp. 173-195, p. 184.)

[9] Carrington, W., 'Experiments in the Paranormal Cognition of Drawings', *IV Proc. S.P.R.*, XLVII, 1941-1945, pp. 150-228, p. 193.

[10] Cohen, M. R., *Reason and Nature*, Harcourt Brace, New York, 1931, p. xiii. Just as there is a large grain of truth in the old statement that all Western philosophy is a series of footnotes to Plato, there is a similar grain of truth in the idea that all psychical research and parapsychology is a series of footnotes to Frederic Myers. He believed, for example, that in veridical hallucinations (as in deathbed apparitions) the agent

affected changes in space, but not the kind of space that is physical, and not in physical objects. This is very close to the present view that there are different kinds of space and that Type B perceptions take place in psychological space, not physical space. Gardner Murphy has discussed this repeatedly.

11 Stevenson, I., *Telepathic Impressions,* University of Virginia Press, Charlottesville, Va. 1970.

12 Tischner, R., *Telepathy and Clairvoyance,* Kegan, Trench, Trubner and Co., London, 1925, p. 190.

13 Tyrrell, G. N. M., *Apparitions,* Collier, New York, p. 12.

14 James, W., *Human Immortality,* Houghton-Mifflin, Boston, 1898, p. 41.

15 Wilder Penfield, the leading brain physiologist of the present period up to his death in 1976, pointed out the differences between the realm of consciousness and the realm of brain reaction, and the limits of extrapolating from one to the other: 'to expect the highest brain mechanism or any set of reflexes, however complicated, to carry out what the mind does, and thus perform all the functions of the mind is quite absurd.' (Penfield, W., *op. cit.,* p. 71.) He points out, for example, that although stimulation of the cortex by electrical means can cause recall of past events, 'there is no place in the cerebral cortex where electrical stimulation will cause a patient to believe or to decide ... nor bring to pass what could be called "mind action" ' (p. 77).

16 In Max Planck's words: 'You cannot expect a physically meaningful answer to a physically meaningless question.' (Quoted in Rosenthal-Schneider, I., *Reality and Scientific Truth,* Wayne State University Press, Detroit, 1980, p. 98.) Nor can you – and it is here that psychical research and parapsychology have failed to consider the matter clearly – expect a parapsychologically meaningful answer to a psychologically meaningless question. Such as 'How does the information get across the space from one consciousness to another?'

17 'No percipient of telepathy, clairvoyance or precognition, so far as I can gather, has ever been consciously aware of a telepathic, clairvoyant or precognitive *process* at work within him. No one has ever been able to say: Now I am conscious that a telepathic message is coming to me from origin X; or: Now I am aware of the process of clairvoyantly perceiving an object Y; or: Now I am conscious that knowledge of a future event Z is reaching me. It is always the *product* and never the *process* of paranormal cognition of which the subject is aware. In this respect paranormal cognition resembles normal perception and also memory.' Tyrrell, G. N. M., 'The Modus Operandi of Paranormal Cognition', *Proc. S.P.R.,* 1946, part 173, vol. XVIII, p. 67.

6: Parapsychology and the Realm of Meaningful Behaviour

[1] Hall, E. T., *The Hidden Dimension,* Doubleday, New York, 1969, p. 115.

[2] Ibid., and Hall, E. T., *Beyond Culture,* Anchor Doubleday, New York, 1976.

[3] Cassirer, E., *The Philosophy of Symbolic Forms* (R. Manheim, tr.), Yale University Press, New Haven, 1955, vol. 2, p. 81.

[4] Hall, E. T., *The Hidden Dimension,* p. 118.

[5] Auden, W. H., *Prologue: The Birth of Architecture,* quoted in Hall, ibid., p. 112.

[6] Murphy, G., 'A Carringtonian Approach to Reincarnation Cases', *J.A.S.P.R.,* 67, 1973, pp. 117-129, p. 119.

[7] Rhine, J. B., 'Telepathy and Human Personality', *J.P.* 25, 1951, pp. 6-39, p. 20.

[8] Hall, *The Hidden Dimension,* p. 117.

[9] Roll, W. G., 'The Interpersonal Field of Gardner Murphy', *Theta,* vol. 7, no. 4, Fall 1979, pp. 1-4, p. 2.

[10] Roll, *ibid.*

[11] Hall, *The Hidden Dimension,* p. 93.

[12] Hardin, G., *Exploring the New Ethics for Survival: The Voyage of the Spaceship 'Beagle',* Viking, New York, 1972.

[13] Byers, P., 'Nonverbal communication and ESP', in Shapin, B., and Coly, L. (eds.), Parapsychology Foundations, New York, 1980, pp. 61-65, p. 62.

[14] Birdwhistell, R. L., quoted in Byers, *op. cit.,* p. 63.

[15] Stern, D. M., 'Mother and Infant at Play: The Dyadic Interaction involving facial, vocal and gaze behaviour', in Lewis, M., and Rosenblum, L. (eds.), *The Effect of the Infant on the Caregiver,* Wiley, New York, 1974.

[16] Smith, D. R., and Williamson, L. K., *Interpersonal Communication,* William C. Brown, Publ., Dubuque, Iowa, 1979, p. 22ff.

[17] Birdwhistell, R. L., *Kinetics and Content,* University of Pennsylvania Press, Philadelphia, 1970, p. 12.

[18] Kreitler, H., and Kreitler, S., 'ESP and Cognition', *J.P.,* 38, 1974, pp. 247-265, p. 262.

[19] Smith and Williamson, *op. cit.,* p. 74.

[20] *Ibid.,* p. 29.

[21] *Ibid.,* p. 17.

[22] *Ibid.,* p. 20.

[23] *Ibid.,* p. 79.

[24] *Ibid.,* p. 12.

[25] I am indebted to the parapsychologist Robert Morris for calling my attention to an analysis of the various uses of the word 'communication'. This analysis, by D. Mackay, describes five uses.

1. A correlation between Events A and B.
2. A causal interaction between Events A and B.
3. A transmission of information between A and B, regardless of the existence of a 'sender' or 'receiver'.
4. An action by Organism A affecting Organism B.
5. A transaction between Organisms A and B.

Each of these is a subset of the one preceding it.

Largely because of their historical development, parapsychologists have been using the first four definitions. Often they have been used as if they were interchangeable and with a complete lack of theoretical clarity. It is high time we moved to the fifth definition.

[26] Byers, P., 'From Biological Rhythm to Cultural Pattern: A Study of Minimal Units', Unpublished Ph.D. thesis, Columbia University, 1972, p. 19.

[27] Hall, E. T., *The Dance of Life,* Anchor Doubleday, New York, 1983.

[28] Birdwhistell, R., 'The Kinesics level in the Investigation of the Emotions in Man', in Knapp, P. H. (ed.), *The Expression of the Emotions in Man,* International Universities Press, New York, 1964, p. 128.

[29] Rhine, L., 'The Way it Looks', *Proc. S.P.R.,* 56, 1982, pp. 367-383.

[30] Byers, *op. cit.,* 1972.

7: Are Paranormal Occurrences Impossible?

[1] Personal communication from Anne Appelbaum, who was present at the meeting.

[2] Hume, D., essay, 'Of Miracles', in *Essays Moral, Political and Literary,* Oxford University Press, 1963.

[3] Inglis, B., *Natural and Supernatural,* Hodder and Stoughton, London, 1977, p. 61.

[4] Hume, D., *An Inquiry Concerning Human Understanding,* 1748.

[5] 'The idea that there is a hard little lump there which *is* the electron or proton, is an illegitimate intrusion of the common sense notions derived from touch . . .' (Russell, B., *An Outline of Philosophy,* 1927, p. 163.)

[6] Margenau, H., *The Nature of Physical Reality,* New York, McGraw Hill, 1950, p. 194.

[7] LeShan, L., *The Medium, the Mystic and the Physicist,* Viking, New York, 1974 (reprinted as *Clairvoyant Reality* [Turnstone Press, 1980], and *Alternate Realities,* Evans, New York, 1976.

[8] Radhakrishnan, S.,*Eastern Religions and Western Thought,* 2nd edition, Oxford University Press, Oxford, 1975.

[9] This paragraph is a paraphrase of some comments of P. W. Bridgman in his *The Logic of Modern Physics,* Macmillan, New York, 1960, p. 46.

8: Type B Perceptions and Human Relationships

[1] A good portion of the following chapter was written with Henry Margenau and originally appeared in the *Journal of the Society for Psychical Research,* vol. 50, March 1980.

[2] Fuller, J. G., *The Airmen Who Would not Die,* G. P. Putnam, New York, 1979.

[3] It is *not* relevant, for example, in astronomy or palaeontology.

[4] Actually this is a far more complex matter than the cavalier treatment given here would indicate. For a fuller discussion, see Margenau, H., *The Nature of Physical Reality,* McGraw-Hill, 1950; Oxbow, New Haven, 1979.

It is only very recently that Honorton has pointed out that parapsychology is concerned with detectable psi, and not with psi *per se.* Honorton, C., 'Psi and Internal Attention States', in Shapin, S., and Coly, L. (eds.), *Psi and States of Awareness,* Parapsychology Foundation, New York, 1978.

[5] To be sure, physicists do occasionally ask this question and they would be likely to answer: 'Gravity is a distortion of the metric of space.' But this is hardly an ultimate answer in any ontological sense. For we would continue to ask, 'What is space?' 'What is . . .' leads to a sequence of answers, none of which will satisfy the ontologist and which, when analyzed, will merely present how one observable relates to others within the domain in question.

The procedures for determining validity of relations between observables in the physical sciences are presented in detail in Margenau, H., *The Nature of Physical Reality,* Oxbow Press, New Haven, 1977. Some of the rules of correspondence leading directly to quantitative observables are not applicable here.

[6] Ehrenwald, J., 'Psi Phenomena: Hemispheric Dominance and the Existential Shift', in Shapin and Coly.

[7] Rhine, L., 'The Way it Looks', *Proc. S.P.R.,* 51, 1982, pp. 367-383.

[8] See, for example, recent volumes of the *Journal of Parapsychology.*

[9] There have been, of course, a great many serious attempts to make the study of this type of event scientific. These include the surveys of the frequency of the phenomena made early in this century. Louisa Rhine's classification system for these occurrences, G. Pratt's quantifications of mediumistically produced materials, G. Schmeidler's research on personality dynamics and psi, R. White's work on the methods of psychics, W. Roll's work on psi fields, and many others. It did not seem possible, however, to find a way to follow the scientific model through consistently.

[10] Johnston, J. C., and McClelland, J. L., 'Perception of Letters in Words: Seek Not and Ye Shall Find, *Science,* 184, June 14 1974, pp. 1192-1193.

[11] Abel, R., *Man is the Measure,* Free Press, New York, 1976, p. 29.

[12] Rhine, L. E., 'The Range of ESP: Limited or Unlimited', *J.A.S.P.R.,* 60, 1969, pp. 125-136, p. 135.

[13] McConnell, R. A., 'Research at three levels of Method', *Journal of Parapsychology,* 30, 1966, pp. 195-207, p. 199.

[14] Stevenson, I., *Telepathic Impressions,* University of Virginia Press, Charlottesville, Va., 1970, p. 178.

[15] Olmstead, M. S., *The Small Group,* Random House, New York, 1950, p. 112. Elsewhere, 'group cohesiveness refers to the degree to which members desire to remain in the group'. As is customary in the social sciences, the terms 'force' and 'field of forces' are used in a wider sense than they are in physics.

[16] Cartright, D., 'The Nature of Group Cohesiveness', in Cartright, D., and Zander, A. (eds.), *Group Dynamics,* 3rd ed., Harper and Row, New York, 1968, pp. 91-101.

[17] Sargent, C., personal communication, April 1978. This hypothesis that psi-occurrences are more frequent between people who like each other than between people who do not, is far from a new idea in the field. We are concerned here more with a general system for developing testable hypotheses than with whether these hypotheses are old or new.

[18] Smith, D. R. and Williamson, L. K., *Interpersonal Communication,* William C. Brown, Publ., Dubuque, Iowa, 1977, pp. 14ff.

[19] Bayles, R. F., *Interaction Process Analysis,* Addison-Wesley Press, Cambridge, 1950.

[20] 'There is one area where the conclusions drawn from ESP studies are largely consistent with what we have learned from other topics. This common area deals with the personality dynamics of ESP success and failure.' (Schmeidler, G. R., and McConnell, R. A., *ESP and Personality Patterns,* Yale University Press, New Haven, 1958, p. 4.)

[21] It is well known that babies raised by Parisians grow up with the identity and self-awareness of French city dwellers, and that the same relationship is true in Eskimo and Yorkshire homes. 'A society without members, or individuals without socialization cannot exist. Although they can be analyzed separately, the two are indistinguishable in nature.' (McGee, R., *Points of Departure: Basic Concepts in Sociology,* Dryden Press, Hinsdale, Ill., 1973, p. 99.)

[22] Without identity, I cannot relate. There can be no real 'yes' unless there is also the possibility of a 'no'.

[23] Lindner, D. W., *Psychological Dimensions of Social Interaction,* Addison-Wesley, Reading, Mass., 1973, p. 9ff.

[24] Erikson, E., 'Identity and uprootedness in our time', in Ruitenbeek, H. M., *Varieties of Modern Social Theory,* Dutton, New York, 1963, pp. 55-68.

[25] In the language used here a *'Gestalt'* is a set of interrelated observables in the same sense in which a 'state' of a physical system is defined as a combination of observables.

[26] Cassirer, E., *The Philosophy of Symbolic Forms,* Yale University Press, 1955; *Language and Myth,* Harper, New York, 1940.

[27] The term 'need-determined' may remind the reader of the old tale concerning a father who told his son a bedtime story. A bear was chasing a dog. The dog, in final desperation, climbed a tree and saved his life. The boy looked doubtfully at his father and said: 'But daddy, dogs can't climb trees.' Whereupon the father, pounding the side of the bed, replied: 'This one did. He *had to!*' Here the tale ends.

[28] For background on this problem, see LeShan, L., 'The Purpose of Psi', *J.S.P.R.,* 1977, 49, pp. 637-643.

[29] Personal communication by daughter Ann Cassirer Appelbaum.

[30] LeShan, E., *Living Your Life,* Harper and Row, 1982.

[31] This is a meditation form that can be quite upsetting if done without proper preparation. It should not be done as a 'mind-game'. It is a very serious procedure. To my knowledge, it was devised by a group in Benares, India, who call themselves 'The Makers of Fords through the River Between the Two Worlds'. I am indebted to Robert Ashby for this information.

[32] LeShan, L., 'A "Spontaneous" Psychometry Experiment with Mrs Eileen Garrett', *J.S.P.R.,* vol. 44, no. 6, 1970, pp. 14-19.

9: On One Aspect of the Realm of Consciousness

[1] Hendel, C. W., in Introduction to Penfield, W., *The Mystery of the Mind,* Princeton University Press, Princeton, N.J., 1975, p. xxii. 'Metaphysics means nothing but an unusually obstinate attempt to think clearly.' (William James.)

[2] Murphy, G., 'Triumphs and Defeats in the Study of Mediumship', *J.A.S.P.R.,* LI, 1957, 125-135, p. 130.

[3] Although biological death does not change the history we have with someone, the passage of time may. After death, time 'fades out' our memory of the history, and changes it for us. The history becomes less sharp and real. This may relate to the fact – so often noted in psychical research – that 'communicators' in mediumistic sessions tend to be much more defined and to produce much more evidential material for the first few years after their biological death than after these years. Somewhere between three and seven years after the death, the quality of the communications usually begins to deteriorate.

[4] LeShan, L., and Margenau, H., *Einstein's Space and Van Gogh's Sky: Physical Reality and Beyond,* Macmillan, 1983.

One interesting aspect of this is that we make an identification between consciousness and personality. A person may pretend to be unconscious. It is not possible, however, for a person to pretend to be conscious. When we are investigating the problem of the continuation of consciousness after the death of the body, we are investigating the problem of the personality continuing to exist.

10: Consciousness and the Organization of Reality

[1] Haynes, Renée, 'Changing Fashions in Psychical Research in Britain', *Parapsychology Review,* vol. 14, no. 4, July-August 1983, p. 1.

[2] As nearly 100 years of research in psychology have shown us, our perception is as much a creative as a discovery process. Even such perceptions as the length of a line, the shade of a colour, or the size of a coin is, in part, a construct. It is not a simple sensation, but influenced by the subject's past, his present environment, and his beliefs about the future. This can, today, be endlessly illustrated. The size of a coin is judged as larger by adults who were poor as children than it is by people who were well off financially as children. If you cut from a piece of brown-green cloth the shape of a leaf and the shape of a donkey, and then ask people to judge the colour of the pieces, the 'leaf' is judged as more green, and the 'donkey' as more brown, and so on, for hundreds of demonstrations in the professional literature of psychology.

[3] Abel, R., *Man is the Measure,* Free Press, New York, 1976.

[4] LeShan, L., *Alternate Realities,* Evans, New York, 1976.

[5] LeShan, L., and Margenau, H., *Einstein's Space and Van Gogh's Sky: Physical Reality and Beyond,* Macmillan, New York, 1982.

[6] Some of the above is a paraphrase of Berger, P., Berger, B., and Kellner, H., *The Homeless Mind,* Random House, New York, p. 13. See also, Berger, P., *A Rumor of Angels,* Doubleday, New York, 1969.

Will McWhinney of Venice, California, has been applying this concept of four major modes of construing reality to various kinds of interpersonal problems. He reports that using this as the basis for a psychotherapeutic method is achieving a good deal of success.

11: A Research Project in Psychic Healing

[1] Winston, S., 'A Multivariate Experiment in Psychic Healing', Ph.D. thesis, Union Graduate School, 1975.

[2] Goodrich, J., An Experiment in Psychic Healing; Ph.D. thesis, Union Graduate School, 1974.

[3] That this type of assumption must be marked 'Handle with Care' is

illustrated by the old story of the man who got drunk on scotch and water on Monday, gin and water on Tuesday, rye and water on Wednesday, and so on through the week. A scientist investigating his behaviour showed that the common factor was water and that this was what made him drunk.

The assumption made in this research – that the altered state of consciousness was the critical factor in psychic healing – was useful for research purposes. It made it possible to isolate *one of the factors* of a successful healing encounter. Psychic healing is not *caused* by the healer's change of state of consciousness, any more than the spark which occurs when you put a wire from one terminal of your car battery to the other is caused by the positive terminal. This factor is simply one part of a situation which makes a transaction possible between two people, a 'healer' and a 'healee'. Each must be in a state that together makes a transaction occur which changes both of them.

[4] This training procedure was made by analyzing one set of steps – of changes in consciousness – that would lead from the Sensory Mode of organizing reality to the Clairvoyant or Unit Mode. For each step several meditations were selected. (I used the concept that a meditation is a device to change consciousness in a specific way, just as a specific exercise in a gymnasium is a device to change the body.) Meditations were selected for each step either to make that step or to ease the anxiety connected with the change. Several meditations were selected for each step, as no one meditation is valid for everyone.

The process of 'five days of very intensive work' which I designed on this basis seemed to be effective for most people selected. To date, over 400 have been trained. My best estimate is that 80 to 90 per cent have learned how to make this change. However, constant practice is necessary to maintain and increase skill and a large percentage of those trained have not done this.

[5] All evidence from the literature and from our own experience, however, finds no evidence of negative effects, and a good deal of suggestive material that points to it being generally beneficial from a biological and a psychological viewpoint.

[6] LeShan, L., *The Medium, the Mystic and the Physicist,* Viking, New York, 1971. Reprinted as *Clairvoyant Reality,* Turnstone Press, 1980.

[7] Goodrich, *op. cit.*

[8] Winston, *op. cit.*

12: Conclusions and Overture

[1] Matson, F., *The Idea of Man,* Dell, New York, 1970, p. 11.

[2] Haynes, R., *The Seeing Eye, the Seeing I,* Hutchinson, London, 1982, p. 63.

[3] Koch, S., 'The Nature and Limits of Psychological Knowledge', *American Psychologist*, vol. 36, no. 3, March, 1981, pp. 257-269, p. 267.

[4] Cassirer, E., *The Logic of The Humanities*, Yale University Press, New Haven, 1960, p. 144.

[5] Kahn, D., *The Enigma of Parapsychology: A Challenge for Science*. Manuscript in files of Parapsychology Foundation.

The analysis of Galileo's change of the formulation of 'motion' has also been described in detail by the historian Herbert Butterfield (Butterfield, H., *The Origins of Modern Science*, Collier, New York, 1962.)

INDEX